I0492005

Fashion Coloring Book For Adults
For Adults
Adult Color By Number
Fun and Colorful Vogue
Color By Numbers For Adults

by Color Questopia

Copyright © 2020

All rights reserved. No part of this publication may be reproduced, distributed, or transmitted in any form or by any means, including photocopying, recording, or other electronic or mechanical methods, without the prior written permission of the publisher

Thank you
for your purchase!

**Claim your FREE digital copy of our
Highlight Reel Color By Number Book:**

Check out our website: colorquestopia.com

**Join our Facebook group:
facebook.com/colorquestopia**

Follow us on Instagram: @colorquestopia

**Did you enjoy this book?
Please leave us a review!**

https://geni.us/cqreview

Color By Number Tips

1. **Relax and have fun**

   Let your cares slip away as you color the images. Take your time. Coloring is a meditative activity and there's no wrong way to do it. Feel free to color as you listen to music, watch TV, lounge in bed- do whatever relaxes you most! You can also color while you're out and about- on the train or at a cafe- take the book with you anywhere you go. Coloring is therapeutic and is great for stress relief and relaxation!

2. **Colors corresponding to each number are shown on the back cover of the book - THIS BOOK HAS OUR NEW COLORING SYSTEM WHERE EVERY COLOR IN EVERY BOOK IS SHOWN ON THE BACK OF THE BOOK**

   Each number corresponds to a color shown on the back of the book. Because this is our new system, there may be colors and numbers on the back that aren't in this book- that's totally okay. Just follow the numbers on the images in this book, and match those numbers to colors. You can match the color as closely as you like- but feel free to change the color or the shade if you don't have the exact color match- that's totally fine. Although this is a color by number book, it's completely okay to get creative and color the images with whichever colors you like and have. The numbers are there to be a guide and to allow you to color without having to focus your energy on choosing colors.

3. **Choose your coloring tools**

   Everyone has their favorite coloring markers, crayons, pencils, pens- even paints! Feel free to color with any tool that you like! If you choose markers or paints, we recommend putting a blank sheet of paper or cardboard behind each image, so that your colors don't run onto the next image.

1. Black	26. Dark Green
2. Golden	27. Peach
3. Light Red	28. Light Pink
4. Medium Red	29. Medium Pink
5. Red	30. Pink
6. Dark Red	31. Hot Pink
7. Lemon Yellow	32. Dark Pink
8. Light Yellow	33. Medium Purple
9. Yellow	34. Purple
10. Dark Yellow	35. Light Violet
11. Bright Orange	36. Soft Violet
12. Light Orange	37. Violet
13. Medium Orange	38. Dark Violet
14. Orange	39. Baby Blue
15. Dark Orange	40. Sky Blue
16. Chocolate	41. Light Blue
17. Light Brown	42. Medium Blue
18. Medium Brown	43. Blue
19. Brown	44. Dark Blue
20. Dark Brown	45. Navy Blue
21. Neon Green	46. Beige
22. Light Green	47. Light Gray
23. Medium Green	48. Medium Gray
24. Green	49. Gray
25. Army Green	50. Dark Gray

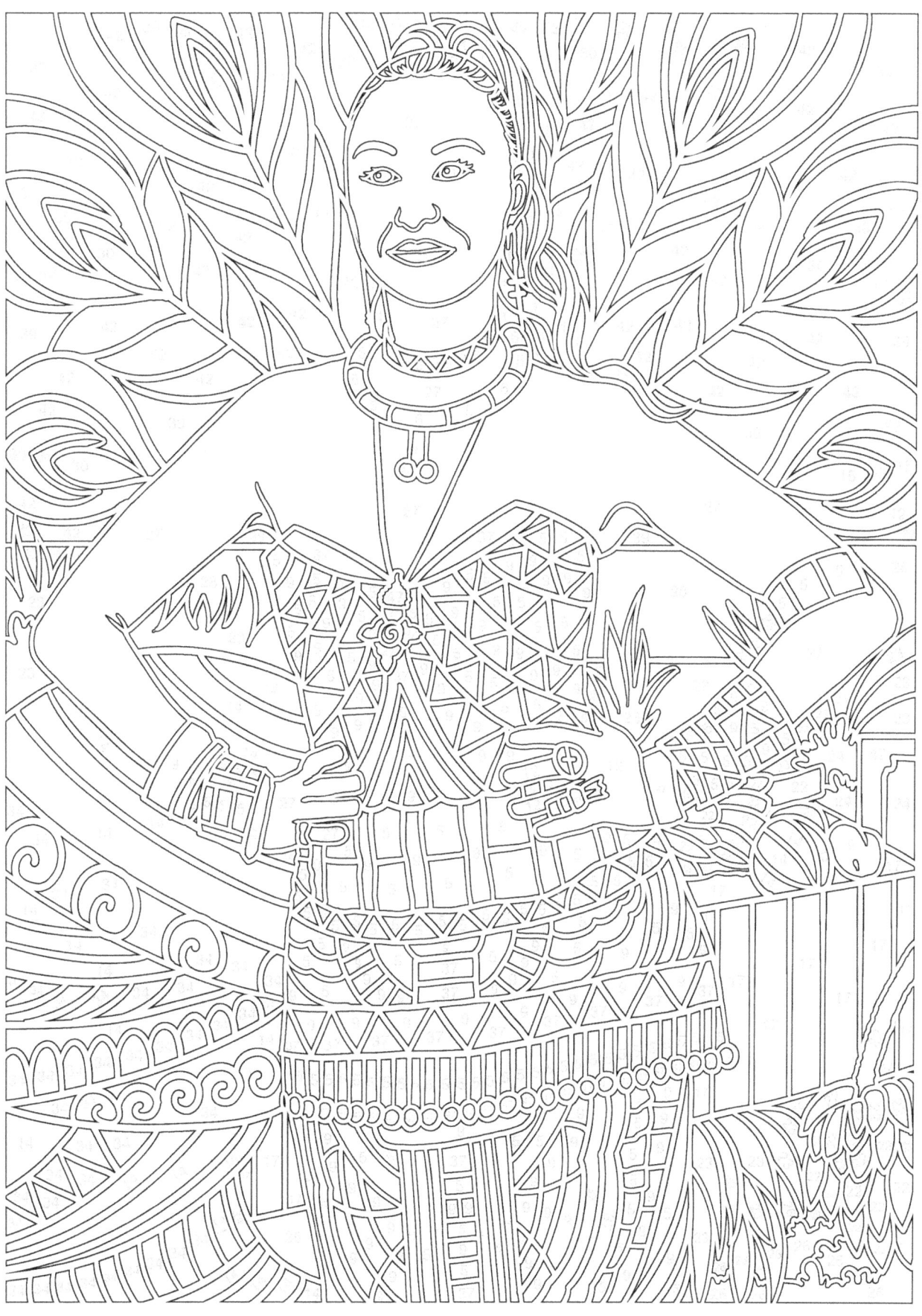

1. Black	26. Dark Green
2. Golden	27. Peach
3. Light Red	28. Light Pink
4. Medium Red	29. Medium Pink
5. Red	30. Pink
6. Dark Red	31. Hot Pink
7. Lemon Yellow	32. Dark Pink
8. Light Yellow	33. Medium Purple
9. Yellow	34. Purple
10. Dark Yellow	35. Light Violet
11. Bright Orange	36. Soft Violet
12. Light Orange	37. Violet
13. Medium Orange	38. Dark Violet
14. Orange	39. Baby Blue
15. Dark Orange	40. Sky Blue
16. Chocolate	41. Light Blue
17. Light Brown	42. Medium Blue
18. Medium Brown	43. Blue
19. Brown	44. Dark Blue
20. Dark Brown	45. Navy Blue
21. Neon Green	46. Beige
22. Light Green	47. Light Gray
23. Medium Green	48. Medium Gray
24. Green	49. Gray
25. Army Green	50. Dark Gray

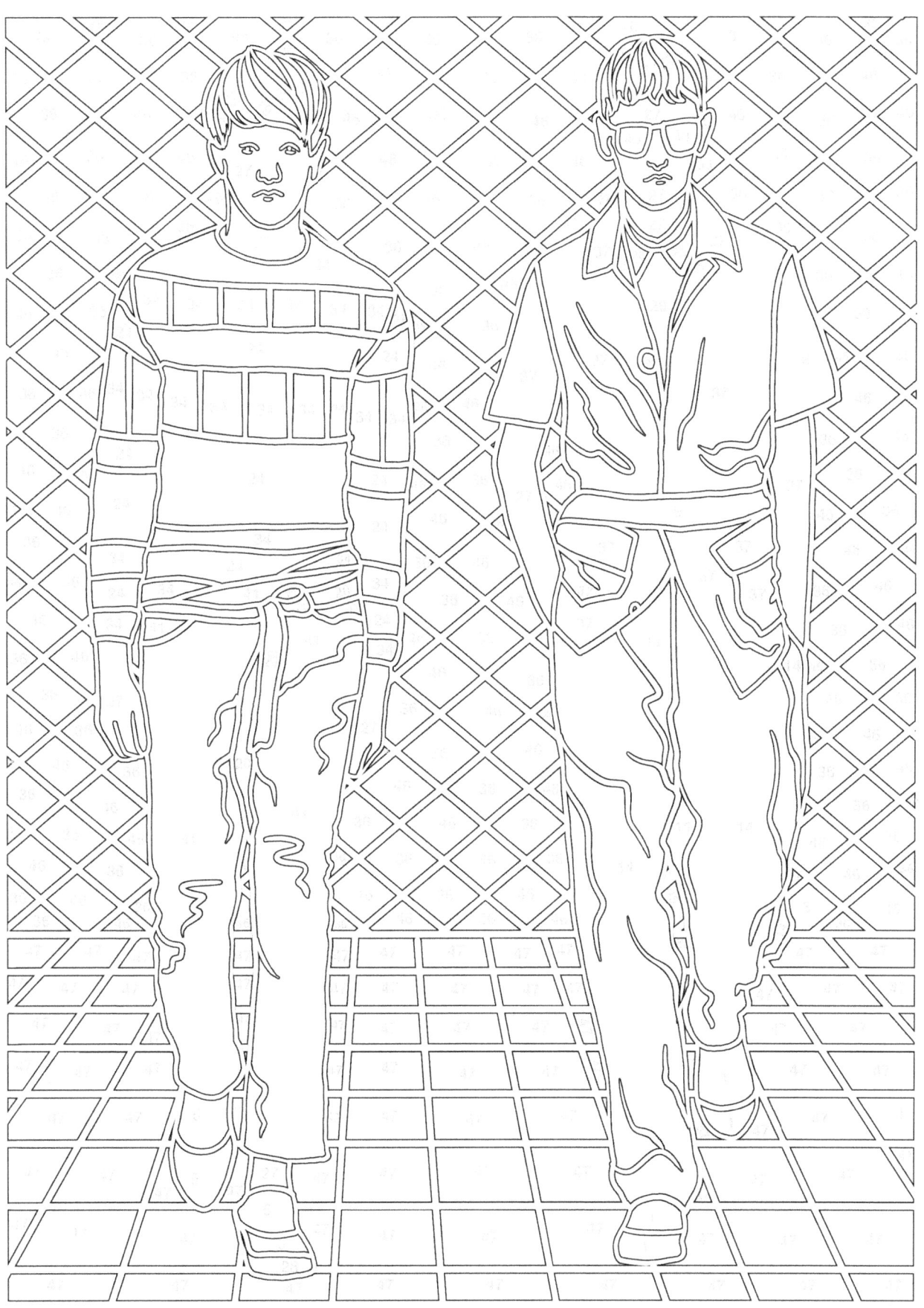

1. Black	26. Dark Green
2. Golden	27. Peach
3. Light Red	28. Light Pink
4. Medium Red	29. Medium Pink
5. Red	30. Pink
6. Dark Red	31. Hot Pink
7. Lemon Yellow	32. Dark Pink
8. Light Yellow	33. Medium Purple
9. Yellow	34. Purple
10. Dark Yellow	35. Light Violet
11. Bright Orange	36. Soft Violet
12. Light Orange	37. Violet
13. Medium Orange	38. Dark Violet
14. Orange	39. Baby Blue
15. Dark Orange	40. Sky Blue
16. Chocolate	41. Light Blue
17. Light Brown	42. Medium Blue
18. Medium Brown	43. Blue
19. Brown	44. Dark Blue
20. Dark Brown	45. Navy Blue
21. Neon Green	46. Beige
22. Light Green	47. Light Gray
23. Medium Green	48. Medium Gray
24. Green	49. Gray
25. Army Green	50. Dark Gray

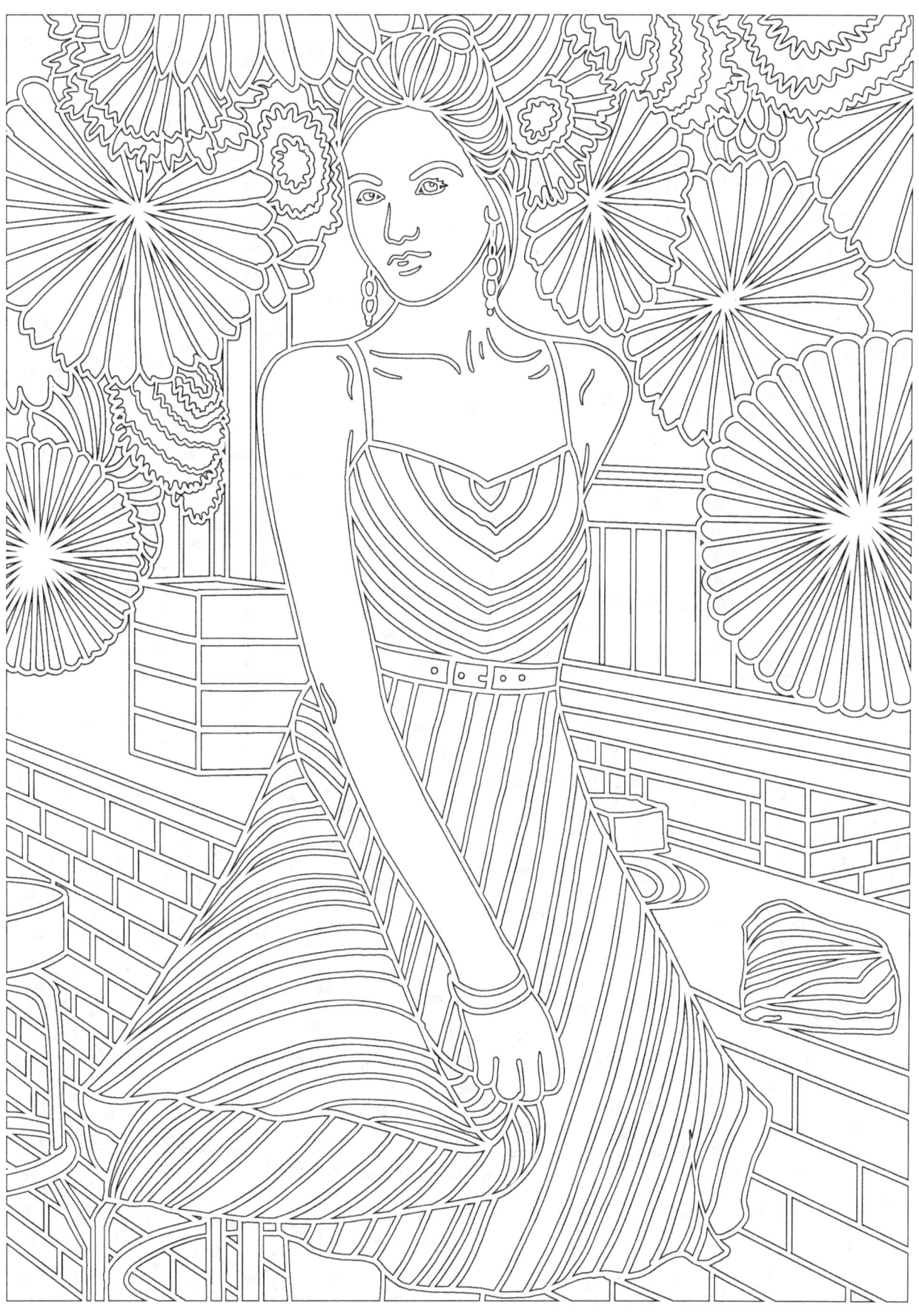

1. Black	26. Dark Green
2. Golden	27. Peach
3. Light Red	28. Light Pink
4. Medium Red	29. Medium Pink
5. Red	30. Pink
6. Dark Red	31. Hot Pink
7. Lemon Yellow	32. Dark Pink
8. Light Yellow	33. Medium Purple
9. Yellow	34. Purple
10. Dark Yellow	35. Light Violet
11. Bright Orange	36. Soft Violet
12. Light Orange	37. Violet
13. Medium Orange	38. Dark Violet
14. Orange	39. Baby Blue
15. Dark Orange	40. Sky Blue
16. Chocolate	41. Light Blue
17. Light Brown	42. Medium Blue
18. Medium Brown	43. Blue
19. Brown	44. Dark Blue
20. Dark Brown	45. Navy Blue
21. Neon Green	46. Beige
22. Light Green	47. Light Gray
23. Medium Green	48. Medium Gray
24. Green	49. Gray
25. Army Green	50. Dark Gray

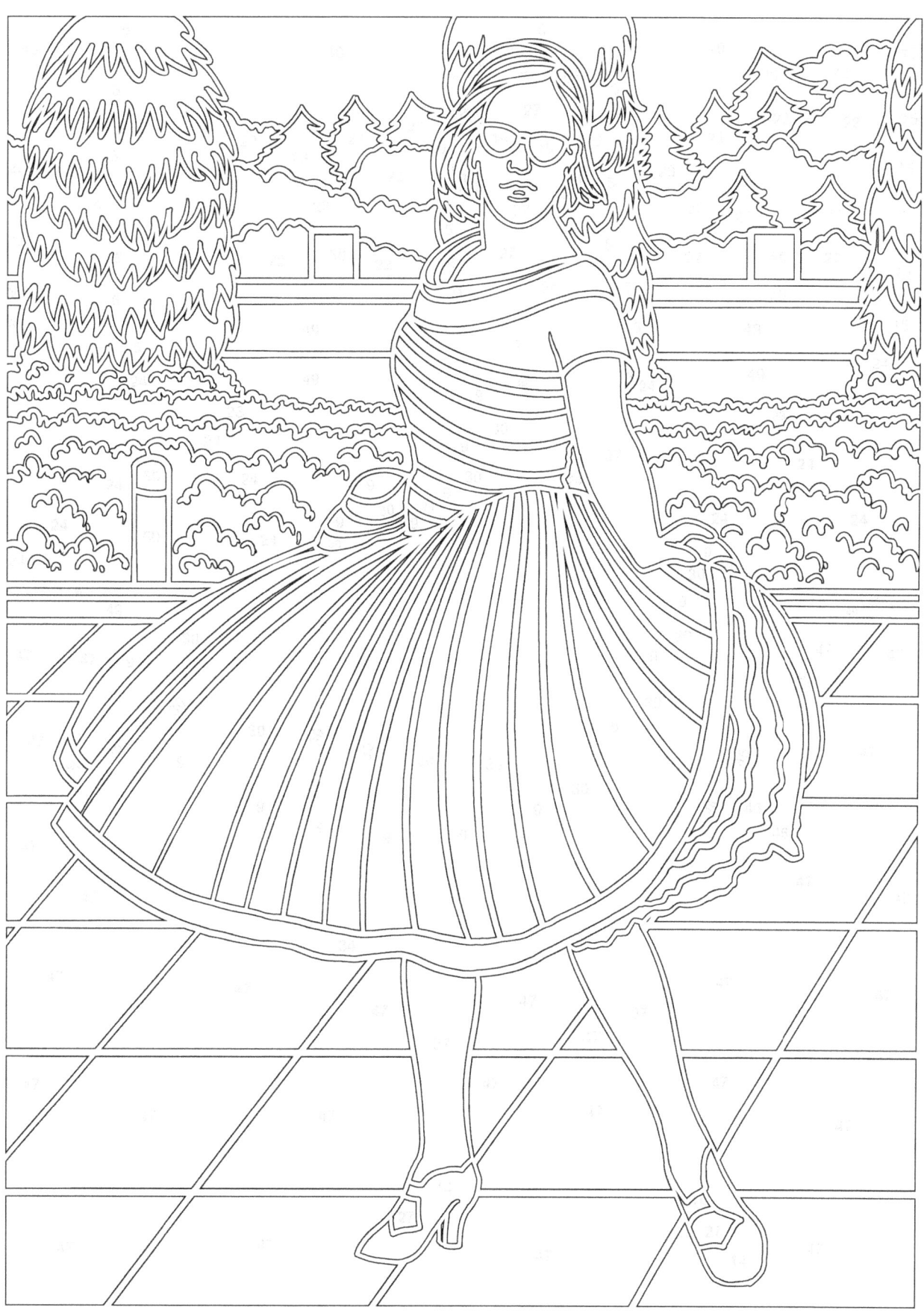

1. Black
2. Golden
3. Light Red
4. Medium Red
5. Red
6. Dark Red
7. Lemon Yellow
8. Light Yellow
9. Yellow
10. Dark Yellow
11. Bright Orange
12. Light Orange
13. Medium Orange
14. Orange
15. Dark Orange
16. Chocolate
17. Light Brown
18. Medium Brown
19. Brown
20. Dark Brown
21. Neon Green
22. Light Green
23. Medium Green
24. Green
25. Army Green
26. Dark Green
27. Peach
28. Light Pink
29. Medium Pink
30. Pink
31. Hot Pink
32. Dark Pink
33. Medium Purple
34. Purple
35. Light Violet
36. Soft Violet
37. Violet
38. Dark Violet
39. Baby Blue
40. Sky Blue
41. Light Blue
42. Medium Blue
43. Blue
44. Dark Blue
45. Navy Blue
46. Beige
47. Light Gray
48. Medium Gray
49. Gray
50. Dark Gray

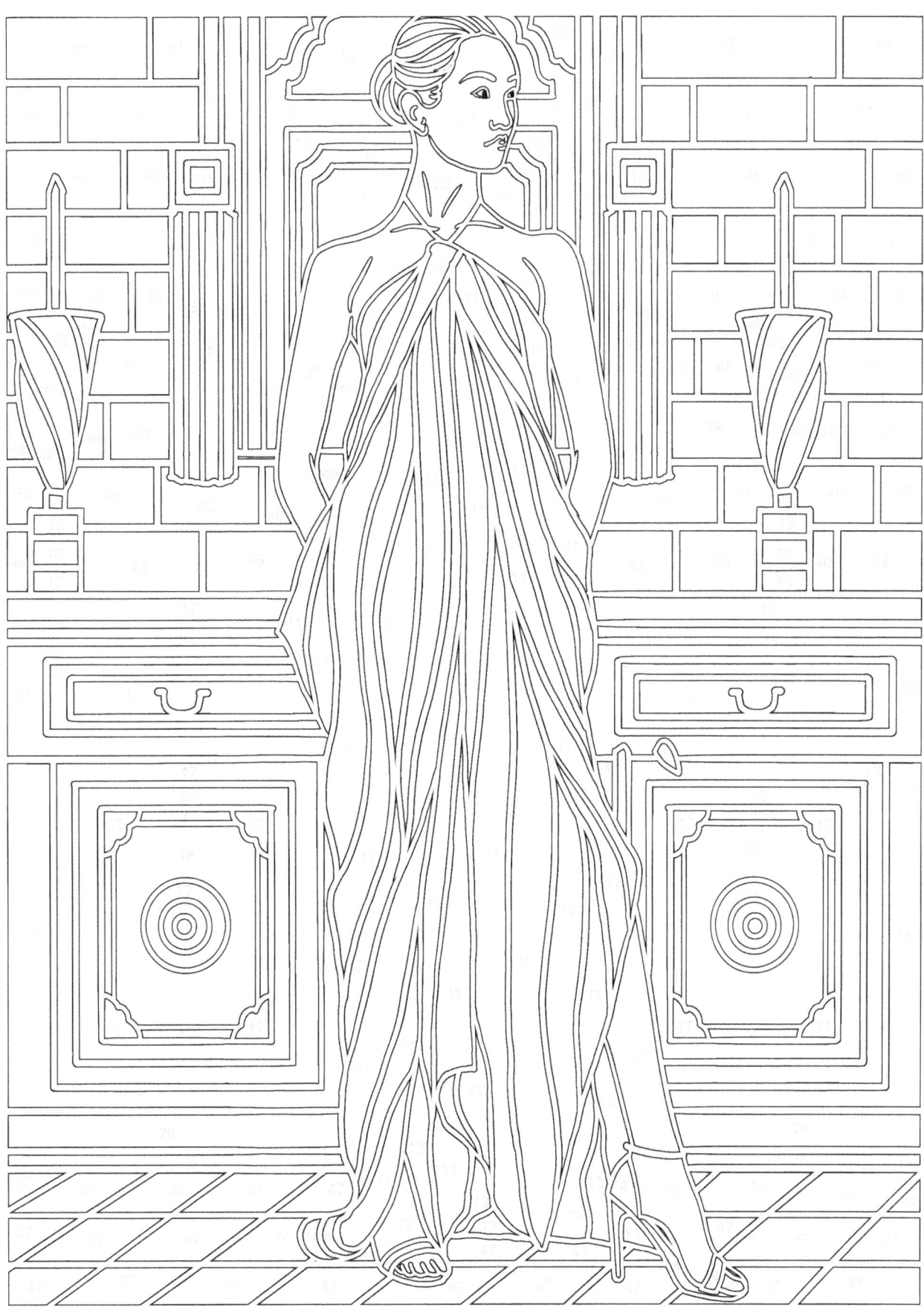

1. Black	26. Dark Green
2. Golden	27. Peach
3. Light Red	28. Light Pink
4. Medium Red	29. Medium Pink
5. Red	30. Pink
6. Dark Red	31. Hot Pink
7. Lemon Yellow	32. Dark Pink
8. Light Yellow	33. Medium Purple
9. Yellow	34. Purple
10. Dark Yellow	35. Light Violet
11. Bright Orange	36. Soft Violet
12. Light Orange	37. Violet
13. Medium Orange	38. Dark Violet
14. Orange	39. Baby Blue
15. Dark Orange	40. Sky Blue
16. Chocolate	41. Light Blue
17. Light Brown	42. Medium Blue
18. Medium Brown	43. Blue
19. Brown	44. Dark Blue
20. Dark Brown	45. Navy Blue
21. Neon Green	46. Beige
22. Light Green	47. Light Gray
23. Medium Green	48. Medium Gray
24. Green	49. Gray
25. Army Green	50. Dark Gray

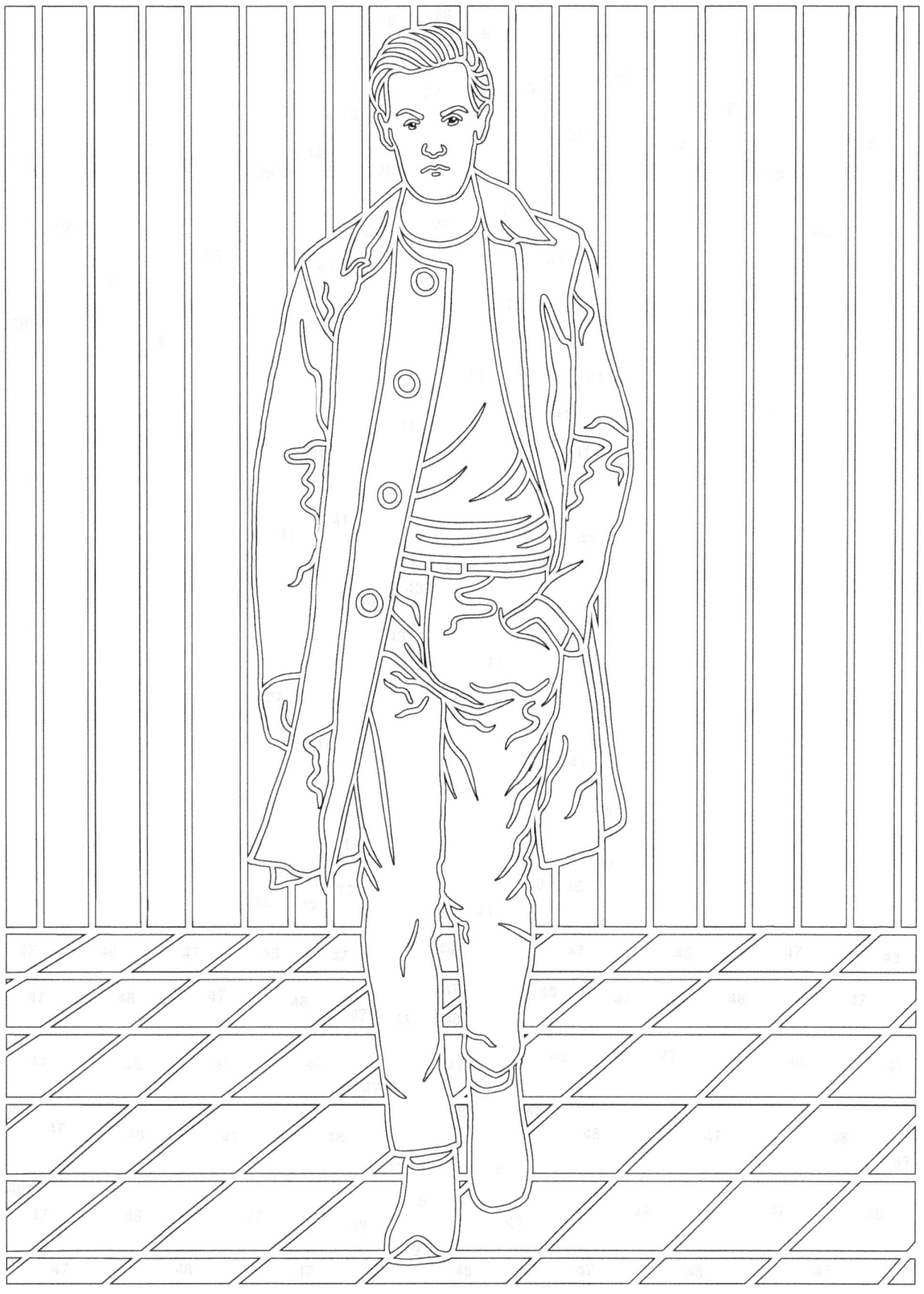

1. Black	26. Dark Green
2. Golden	27. Peach
3. Light Red	28. Light Pink
4. Medium Red	29. Medium Pink
5. Red	30. Pink
6. Dark Red	31. Hot Pink
7. Lemon Yellow	32. Dark Pink
8. Light Yellow	33. Medium Purple
9. Yellow	34. Purple
10. Dark Yellow	35. Light Violet
11. Bright Orange	36. Soft Violet
12. Light Orange	37. Violet
13. Medium Orange	38. Dark Violet
14. Orange	39. Baby Blue
15. Dark Orange	40. Sky Blue
16. Chocolate	41. Light Blue
17. Light Brown	42. Medium Blue
18. Medium Brown	43. Blue
19. Brown	44. Dark Blue
20. Dark Brown	45. Navy Blue
21. Neon Green	46. Beige
22. Light Green	47. Light Gray
23. Medium Green	48. Medium Gray
24. Green	49. Gray
25. Army Green	50. Dark Gray

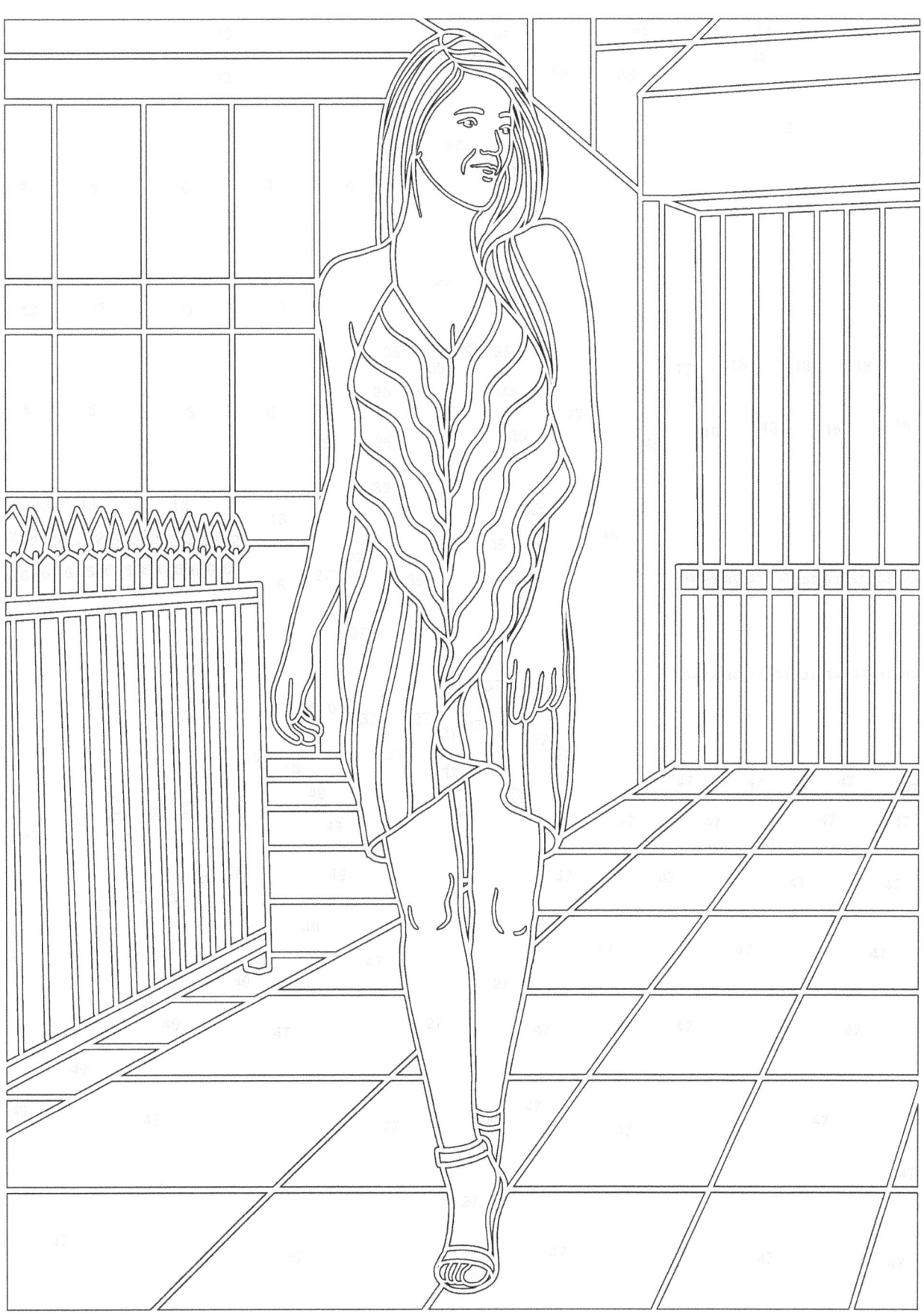

1. Black	26. Dark Green
2. Golden	27. Peach
3. Light Red	28. Light Pink
4. Medium Red	29. Medium Pink
5. Red	30. Pink
6. Dark Red	31. Hot Pink
7. Lemon Yellow	32. Dark Pink
8. Light Yellow	33. Medium Purple
9. Yellow	34. Purple
10. Dark Yellow	35. Light Violet
11. Bright Orange	36. Soft Violet
12. Light Orange	37. Violet
13. Medium Orange	38. Dark Violet
14. Orange	39. Baby Blue
15. Dark Orange	40. Sky Blue
16. Chocolate	41. Light Blue
17. Light Brown	42. Medium Blue
18. Medium Brown	43. Blue
19. Brown	44. Dark Blue
20. Dark Brown	45. Navy Blue
21. Neon Green	46. Beige
22. Light Green	47. Light Gray
23. Medium Green	48. Medium Gray
24. Green	49. Gray
25. Army Green	50. Dark Gray

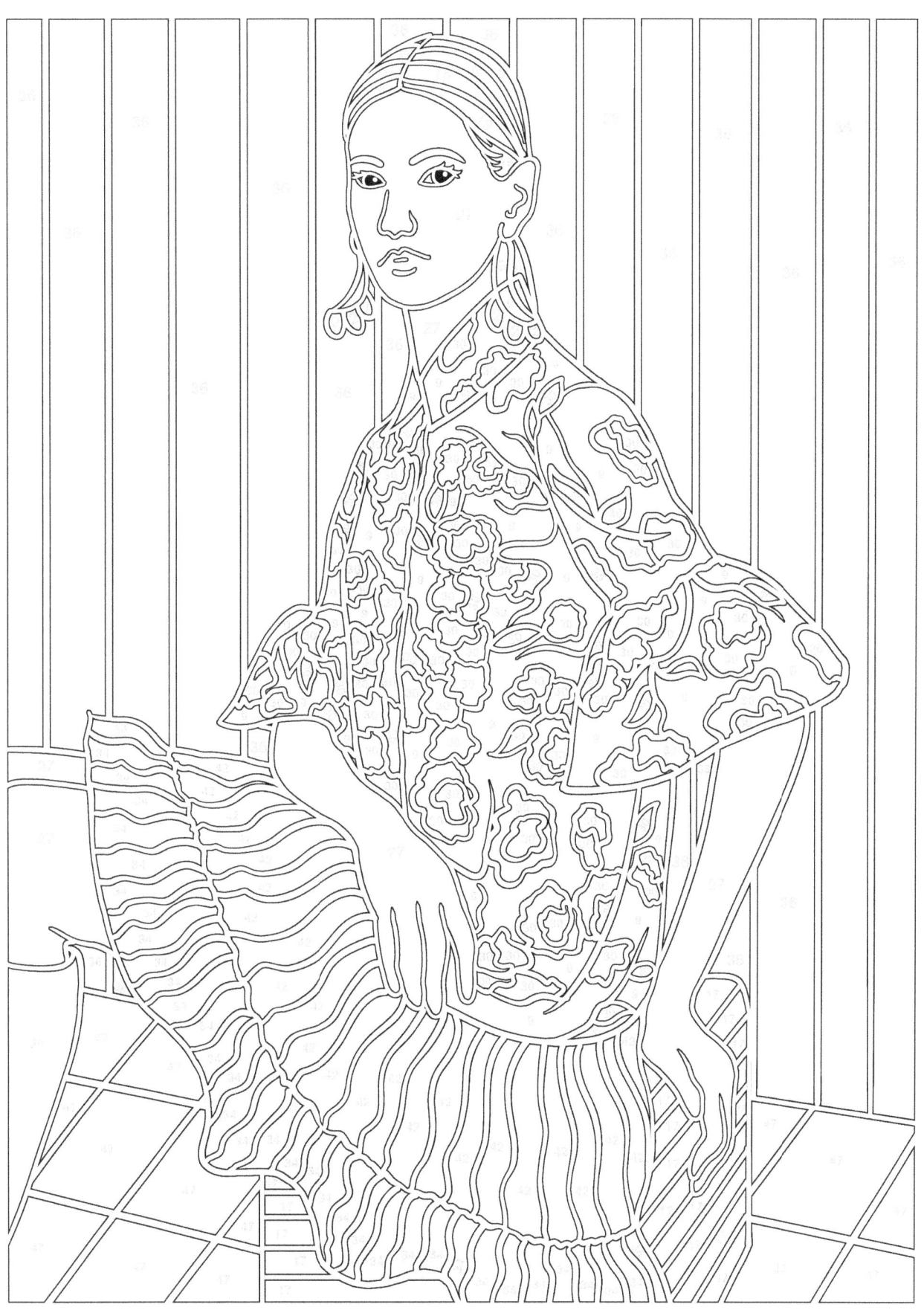

1. Black
2. Golden
3. Light Red
4. Medium Red
5. Red
6. Dark Red
7. Lemon Yellow
8. Light Yellow
9. Yellow
10. Dark Yellow
11. Bright Orange
12. Light Orange
13. Medium Orange
14. Orange
15. Dark Orange
16. Chocolate
17. Light Brown
18. Medium Brown
19. Brown
20. Dark Brown
21. Neon Green
22. Light Green
23. Medium Green
24. Green
25. Army Green
26. Dark Green
27. Peach
28. Light Pink
29. Medium Pink
30. Pink
31. Hot Pink
32. Dark Pink
33. Medium Purple
34. Purple
35. Light Violet
36. Soft Violet
37. Violet
38. Dark Violet
39. Baby Blue
40. Sky Blue
41. Light Blue
42. Medium Blue
43. Blue
44. Dark Blue
45. Navy Blue
46. Beige
47. Light Gray
48. Medium Gray
49. Gray
50. Dark Gray

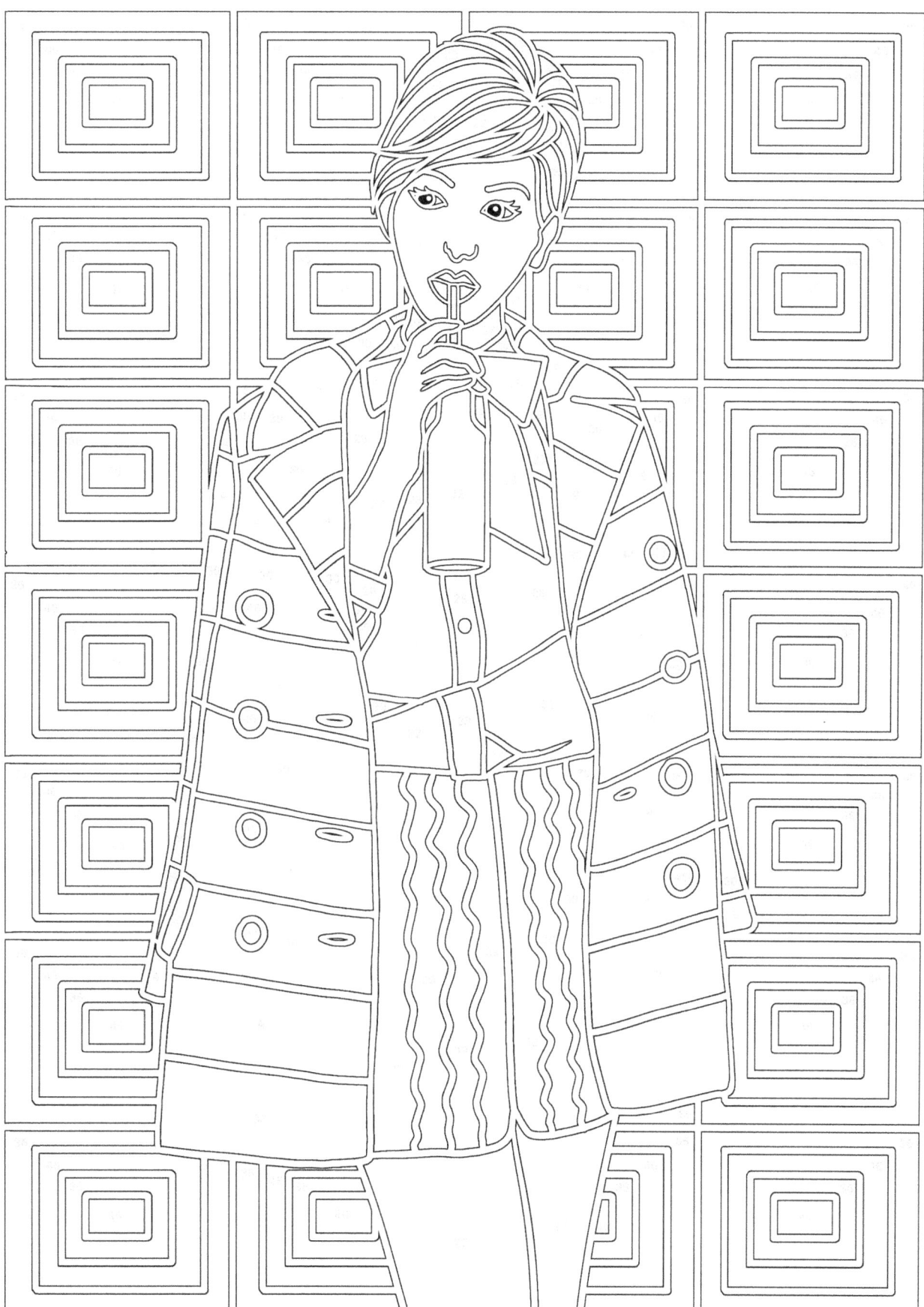

1. Black	26. Dark Green
2. Golden	27. Peach
3. Light Red	28. Light Pink
4. Medium Red	29. Medium Pink
5. Red	30. Pink
6. Dark Red	31. Hot Pink
7. Lemon Yellow	32. Dark Pink
8. Light Yellow	33. Medium Purple
9. Yellow	34. Purple
10. Dark Yellow	35. Light Violet
11. Bright Orange	36. Soft Violet
12. Light Orange	37. Violet
13. Medium Orange	38. Dark Violet
14. Orange	39. Baby Blue
15. Dark Orange	40. Sky Blue
16. Chocolate	41. Light Blue
17. Light Brown	42. Medium Blue
18. Medium Brown	43. Blue
19. Brown	44. Dark Blue
20. Dark Brown	45. Navy Blue
21. Neon Green	46. Beige
22. Light Green	47. Light Gray
23. Medium Green	48. Medium Gray
24. Green	49. Gray
25. Army Green	50. Dark Gray

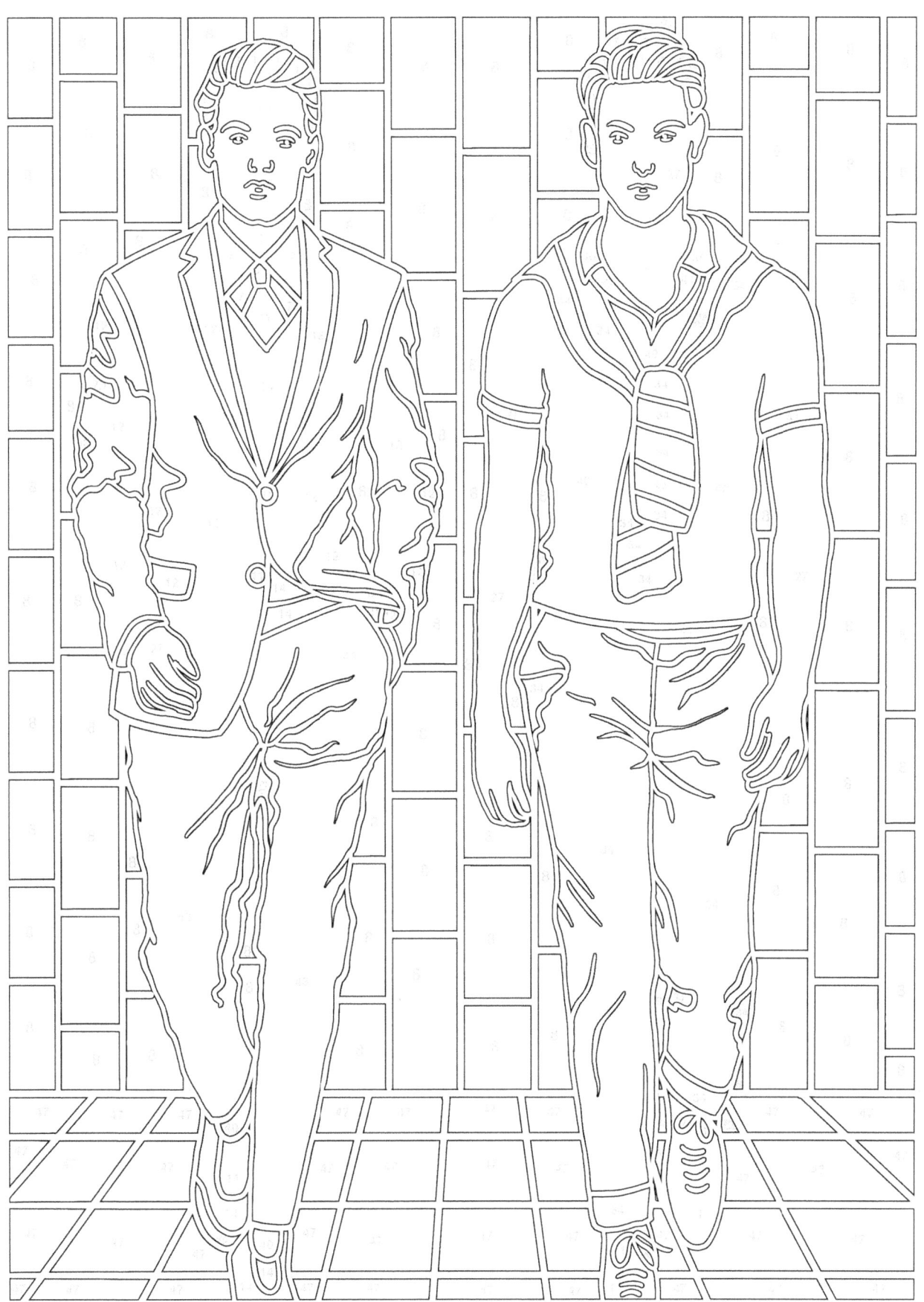

1. Black
2. Golden
3. Light Red
4. Medium Red
5. Red
6. Dark Red
7. Lemon Yellow
8. Light Yellow
9. Yellow
10. Dark Yellow
11. Bright Orange
12. Light Orange
13. Medium Orange
14. Orange
15. Dark Orange
16. Chocolate
17. Light Brown
18. Medium Brown
19. Brown
20. Dark Brown
21. Neon Green
22. Light Green
23. Medium Green
24. Green
25. Army Green
26. Dark Green
27. Peach
28. Light Pink
29. Medium Pink
30. Pink
31. Hot Pink
32. Dark Pink
33. Medium Purple
34. Purple
35. Light Violet
36. Soft Violet
37. Violet
38. Dark Violet
39. Baby Blue
40. Sky Blue
41. Light Blue
42. Medium Blue
43. Blue
44. Dark Blue
45. Navy Blue
46. Beige
47. Light Gray
48. Medium Gray
49. Gray
50. Dark Gray

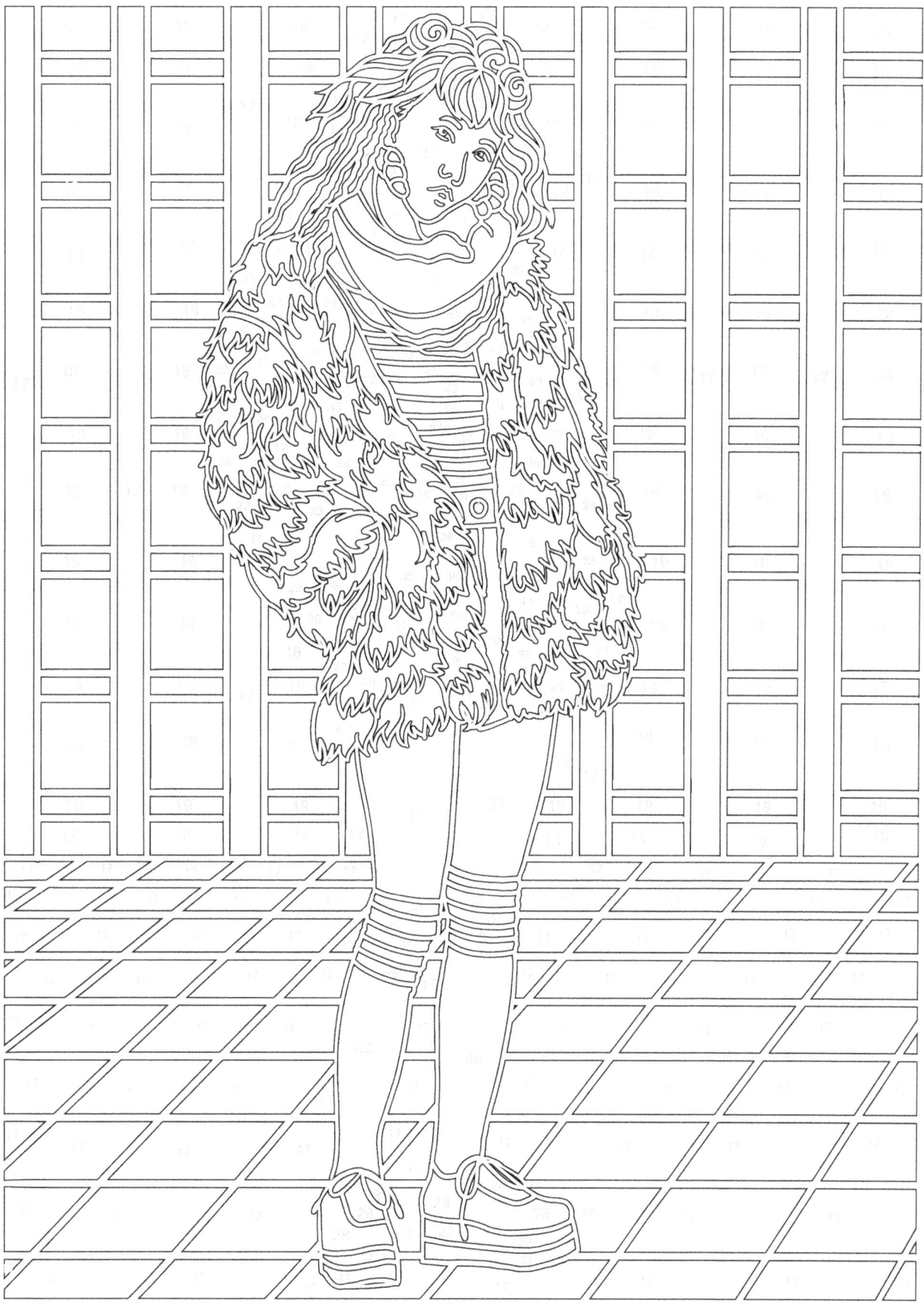

1. Black	26. Dark Green
2. Golden	27. Peach
3. Light Red	28. Light Pink
4. Medium Red	29. Medium Pink
5. Red	30. Pink
6. Dark Red	31. Hot Pink
7. Lemon Yellow	32. Dark Pink
8. Light Yellow	33. Medium Purple
9. Yellow	34. Purple
10. Dark Yellow	35. Light Violet
11. Bright Orange	36. Soft Violet
12. Light Orange	37. Violet
13. Medium Orange	38. Dark Violet
14. Orange	39. Baby Blue
15. Dark Orange	40. Sky Blue
16. Chocolate	41. Light Blue
17. Light Brown	42. Medium Blue
18. Medium Brown	43. Blue
19. Brown	44. Dark Blue
20. Dark Brown	45. Navy Blue
21. Neon Green	46. Beige
22. Light Green	47. Light Gray
23. Medium Green	48. Medium Gray
24. Green	49. Gray
25. Army Green	50. Dark Gray

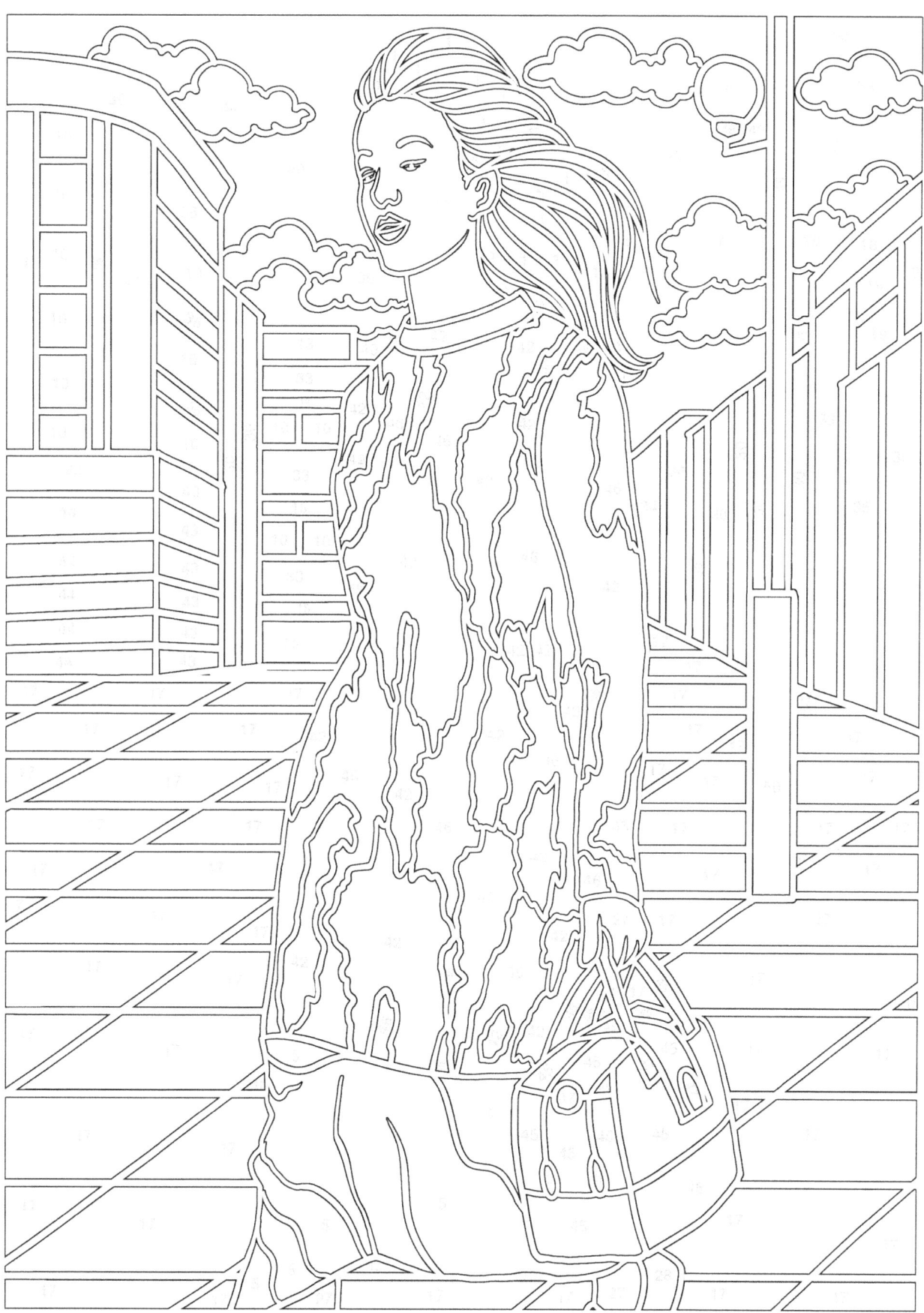

1. Black	26. Dark Green
2. Golden	27. Peach
3. Light Red	28. Light Pink
4. Medium Red	29. Medium Pink
5. Red	30. Pink
6. Dark Red	31. Hot Pink
7. Lemon Yellow	32. Dark Pink
8. Light Yellow	33. Medium Purple
9. Yellow	34. Purple
10. Dark Yellow	35. Light Violet
11. Bright Orange	36. Soft Violet
12. Light Orange	37. Violet
13. Medium Orange	38. Dark Violet
14. Orange	39. Baby Blue
15. Dark Orange	40. Sky Blue
16. Chocolate	41. Light Blue
17. Light Brown	42. Medium Blue
18. Medium Brown	43. Blue
19. Brown	44. Dark Blue
20. Dark Brown	45. Navy Blue
21. Neon Green	46. Beige
22. Light Green	47. Light Gray
23. Medium Green	48. Medium Gray
24. Green	49. Gray
25. Army Green	50. Dark Gray

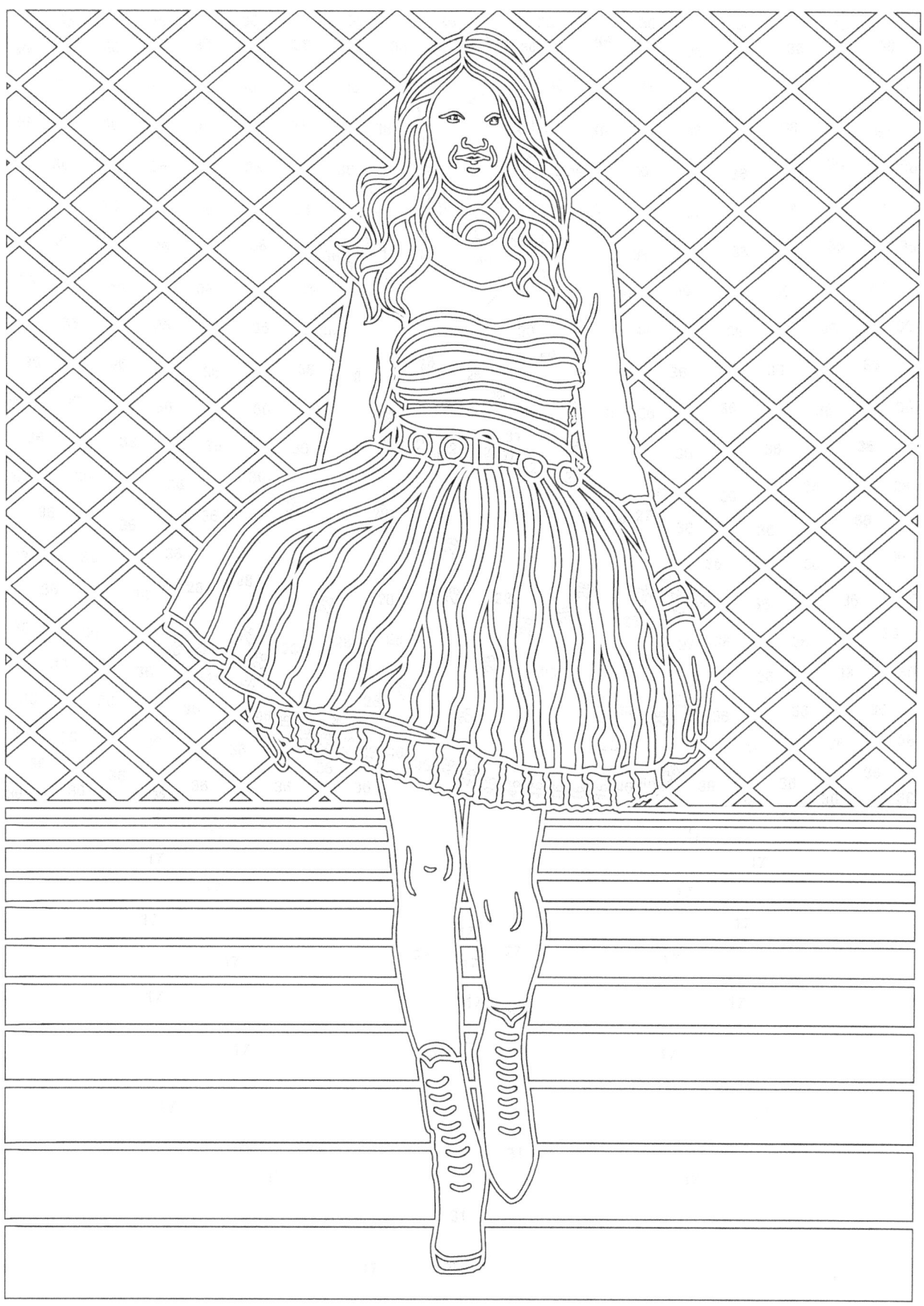

1. Black
2. Golden
3. Light Red
4. Medium Red
5. Red
6. Dark Red
7. Lemon Yellow
8. Light Yellow
9. Yellow
10. Dark Yellow
11. Bright Orange
12. Light Orange
13. Medium Orange
14. Orange
15. Dark Orange
16. Chocolate
17. Light Brown
18. Medium Brown
19. Brown
20. Dark Brown
21. Neon Green
22. Light Green
23. Medium Green
24. Green
25. Army Green
26. Dark Green
27. Peach
28. Light Pink
29. Medium Pink
30. Pink
31. Hot Pink
32. Dark Pink
33. Medium Purple
34. Purple
35. Light Violet
36. Soft Violet
37. Violet
38. Dark Violet
39. Baby Blue
40. Sky Blue
41. Light Blue
42. Medium Blue
43. Blue
44. Dark Blue
45. Navy Blue
46. Beige
47. Light Gray
48. Medium Gray
49. Gray
50. Dark Gray

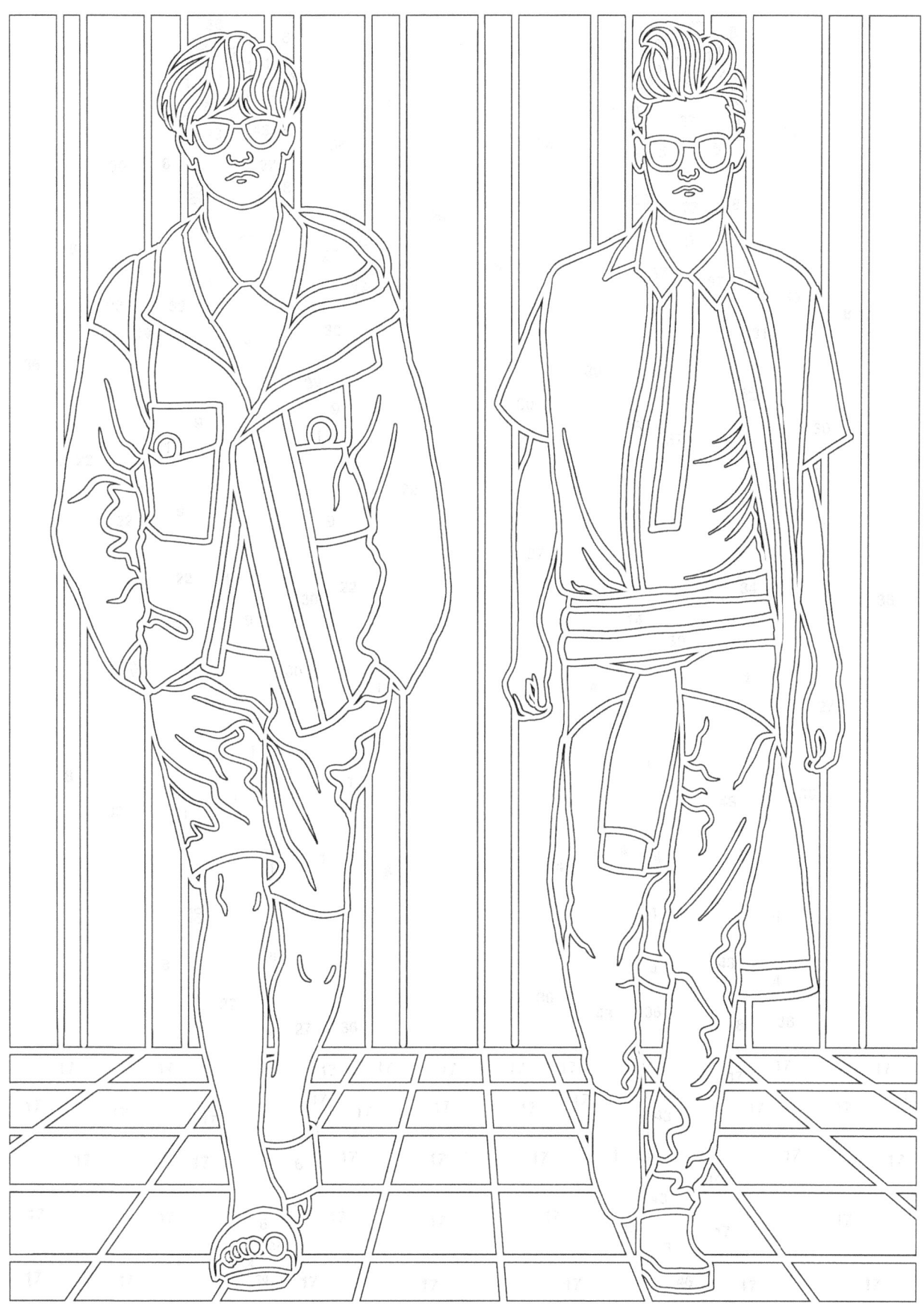

1. Black
2. Golden
3. Light Red
4. Medium Red
5. Red
6. Dark Red
7. Lemon Yellow
8. Light Yellow
9. Yellow
10. Dark Yellow
11. Bright Orange
12. Light Orange
13. Medium Orange
14. Orange
15. Dark Orange
16. Chocolate
17. Light Brown
18. Medium Brown
19. Brown
20. Dark Brown
21. Neon Green
22. Light Green
23. Medium Green
24. Green
25. Army Green
26. Dark Green
27. Peach
28. Light Pink
29. Medium Pink
30. Pink
31. Hot Pink
32. Dark Pink
33. Medium Purple
34. Purple
35. Light Violet
36. Soft Violet
37. Violet
38. Dark Violet
39. Baby Blue
40. Sky Blue
41. Light Blue
42. Medium Blue
43. Blue
44. Dark Blue
45. Navy Blue
46. Beige
47. Light Gray
48. Medium Gray
49. Gray
50. Dark Gray

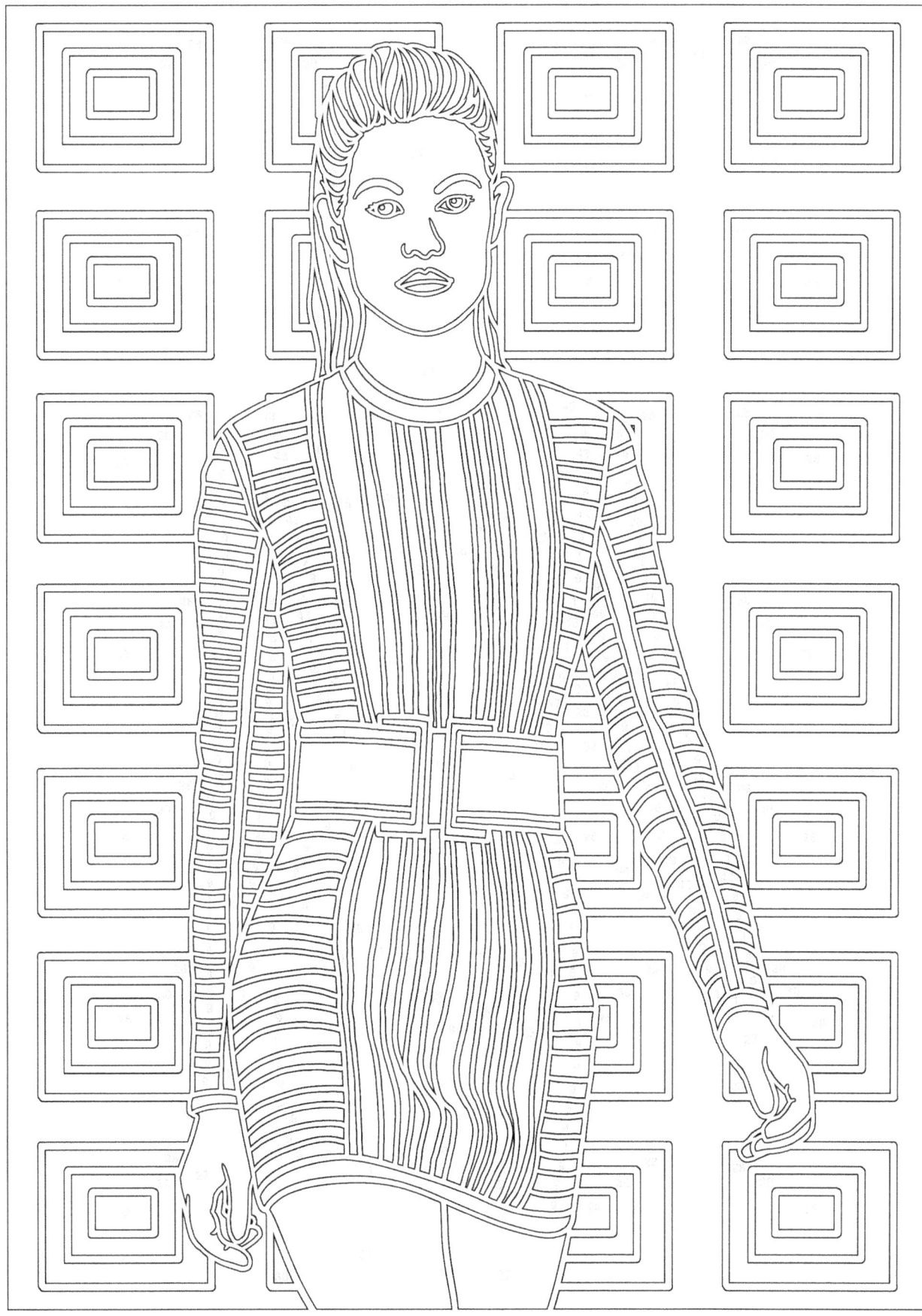

1. Black
2. Golden
3. Light Red
4. Medium Red
5. Red
6. Dark Red
7. Lemon Yellow
8. Light Yellow
9. Yellow
10. Dark Yellow
11. Bright Orange
12. Light Orange
13. Medium Orange
14. Orange
15. Dark Orange
16. Chocolate
17. Light Brown
18. Medium Brown
19. Brown
20. Dark Brown
21. Neon Green
22. Light Green
23. Medium Green
24. Green
25. Army Green
26. Dark Green
27. Peach
28. Light Pink
29. Medium Pink
30. Pink
31. Hot Pink
32. Dark Pink
33. Medium Purple
34. Purple
35. Light Violet
36. Soft Violet
37. Violet
38. Dark Violet
39. Baby Blue
40. Sky Blue
41. Light Blue
42. Medium Blue
43. Blue
44. Dark Blue
45. Navy Blue
46. Beige
47. Light Gray
48. Medium Gray
49. Gray
50. Dark Gray

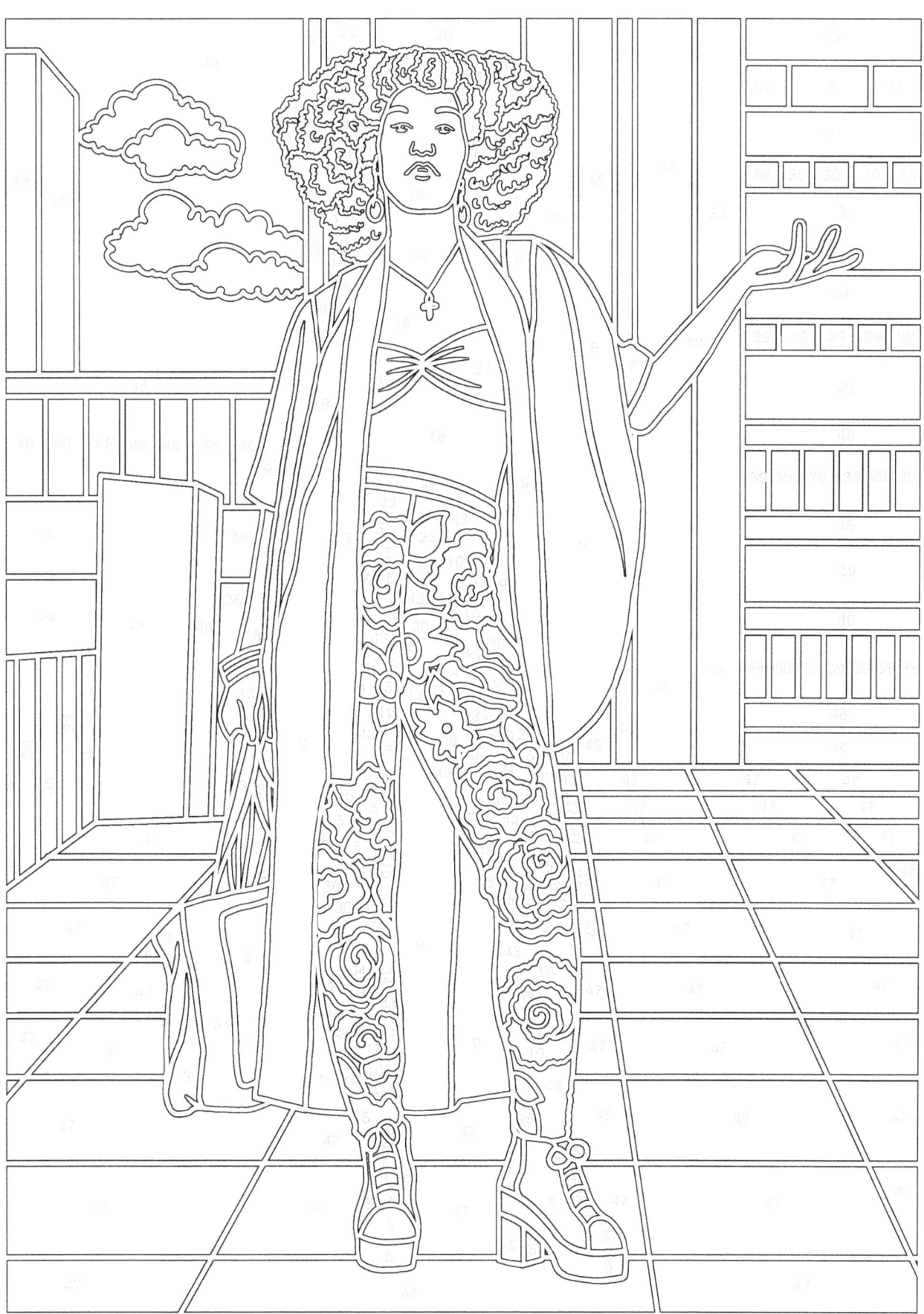

1. Black	26. Dark Green
2. Golden	27. Peach
3. Light Red	28. Light Pink
4. Medium Red	29. Medium Pink
5. Red	30. Pink
6. Dark Red	31. Hot Pink
7. Lemon Yellow	32. Dark Pink
8. Light Yellow	33. Medium Purple
9. Yellow	34. Purple
10. Dark Yellow	35. Light Violet
11. Bright Orange	36. Soft Violet
12. Light Orange	37. Violet
13. Medium Orange	38. Dark Violet
14. Orange	39. Baby Blue
15. Dark Orange	40. Sky Blue
16. Chocolate	41. Light Blue
17. Light Brown	42. Medium Blue
18. Medium Brown	43. Blue
19. Brown	44. Dark Blue
20. Dark Brown	45. Navy Blue
21. Neon Green	46. Beige
22. Light Green	47. Light Gray
23. Medium Green	48. Medium Gray
24. Green	49. Gray
25. Army Green	50. Dark Gray

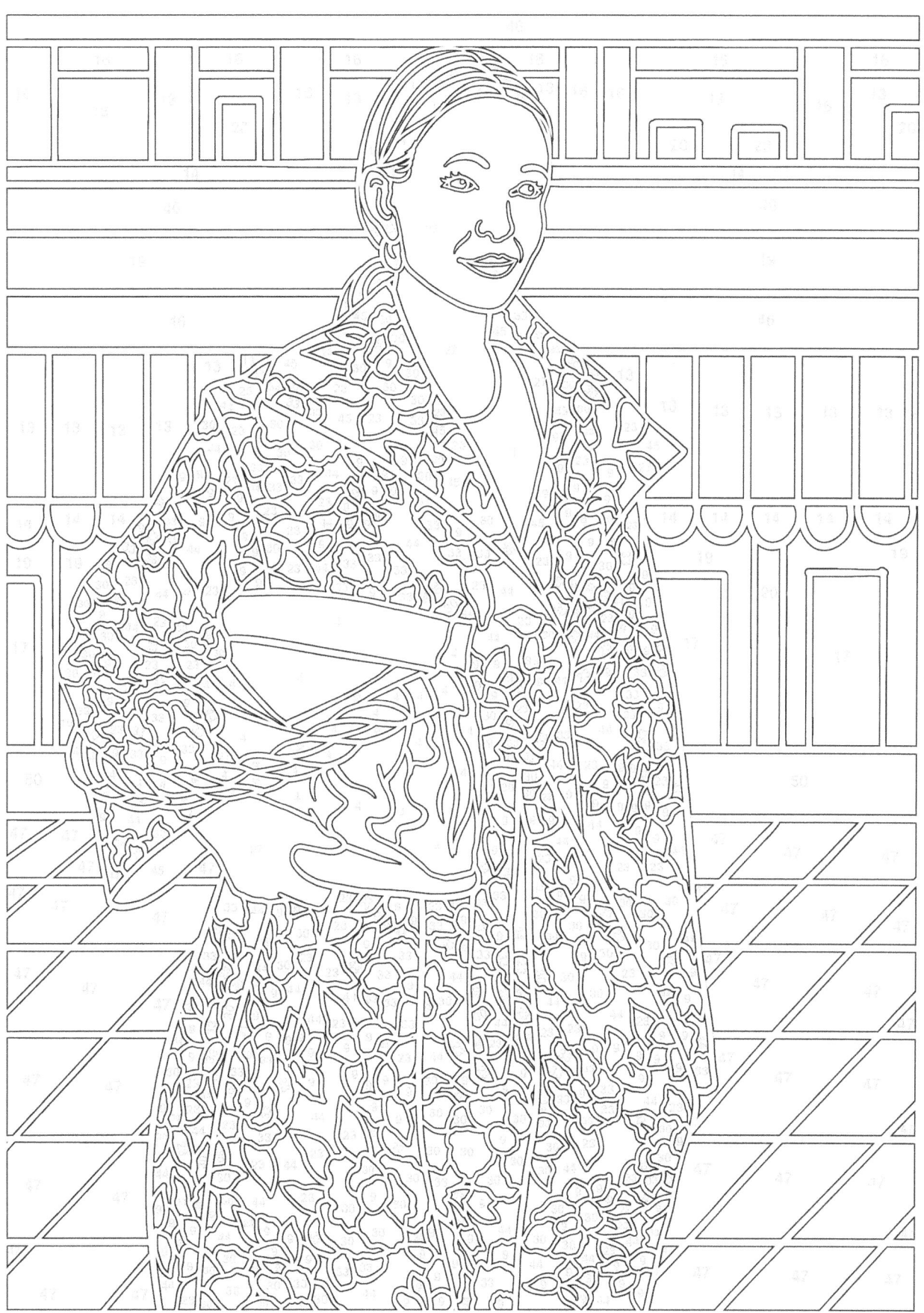

1. Black	26. Dark Green
2. Golden	27. Peach
3. Light Red	28. Light Pink
4. Medium Red	29. Medium Pink
5. Red	30. Pink
6. Dark Red	31. Hot Pink
7. Lemon Yellow	32. Dark Pink
8. Light Yellow	33. Medium Purple
9. Yellow	34. Purple
10. Dark Yellow	35. Light Violet
11. Bright Orange	36. Soft Violet
12. Light Orange	37. Violet
13. Medium Orange	38. Dark Violet
14. Orange	39. Baby Blue
15. Dark Orange	40. Sky Blue
16. Chocolate	41. Light Blue
17. Light Brown	42. Medium Blue
18. Medium Brown	43. Blue
19. Brown	44. Dark Blue
20. Dark Brown	45. Navy Blue
21. Neon Green	46. Beige
22. Light Green	47. Light Gray
23. Medium Green	48. Medium Gray
24. Green	49. Gray
25. Army Green	50. Dark Gray

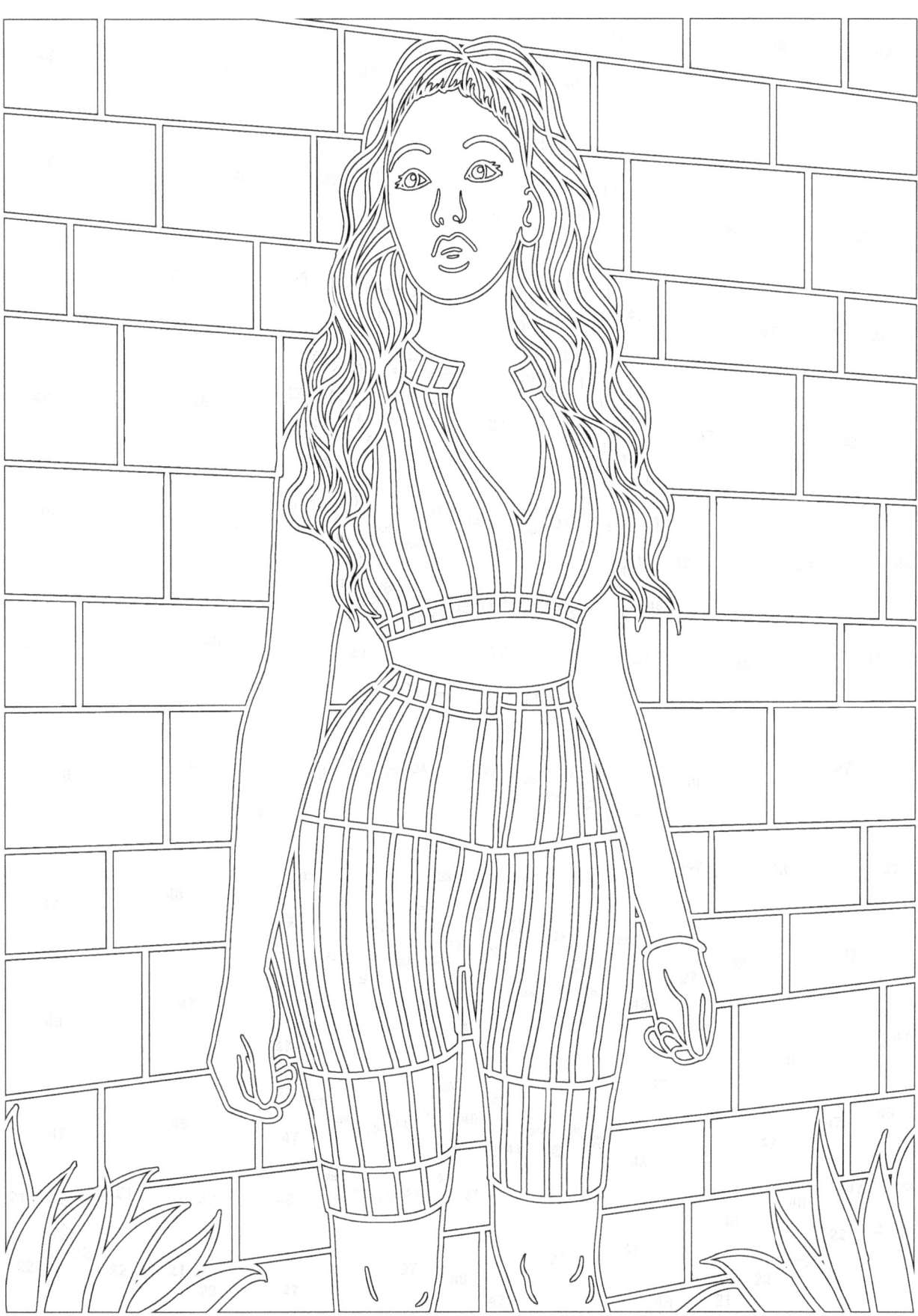

1. Black	26. Dark Green
2. Golden	27. Peach
3. Light Red	28. Light Pink
4. Medium Red	29. Medium Pink
5. Red	30. Pink
6. Dark Red	31. Hot Pink
7. Lemon Yellow	32. Dark Pink
8. Light Yellow	33. Medium Purple
9. Yellow	34. Purple
10. Dark Yellow	35. Light Violet
11. Bright Orange	36. Soft Violet
12. Light Orange	37. Violet
13. Medium Orange	38. Dark Violet
14. Orange	39. Baby Blue
15. Dark Orange	40. Sky Blue
16. Chocolate	41. Light Blue
17. Light Brown	42. Medium Blue
18. Medium Brown	43. Blue
19. Brown	44. Dark Blue
20. Dark Brown	45. Navy Blue
21. Neon Green	46. Beige
22. Light Green	47. Light Gray
23. Medium Green	48. Medium Gray
24. Green	49. Gray
25. Army Green	50. Dark Gray

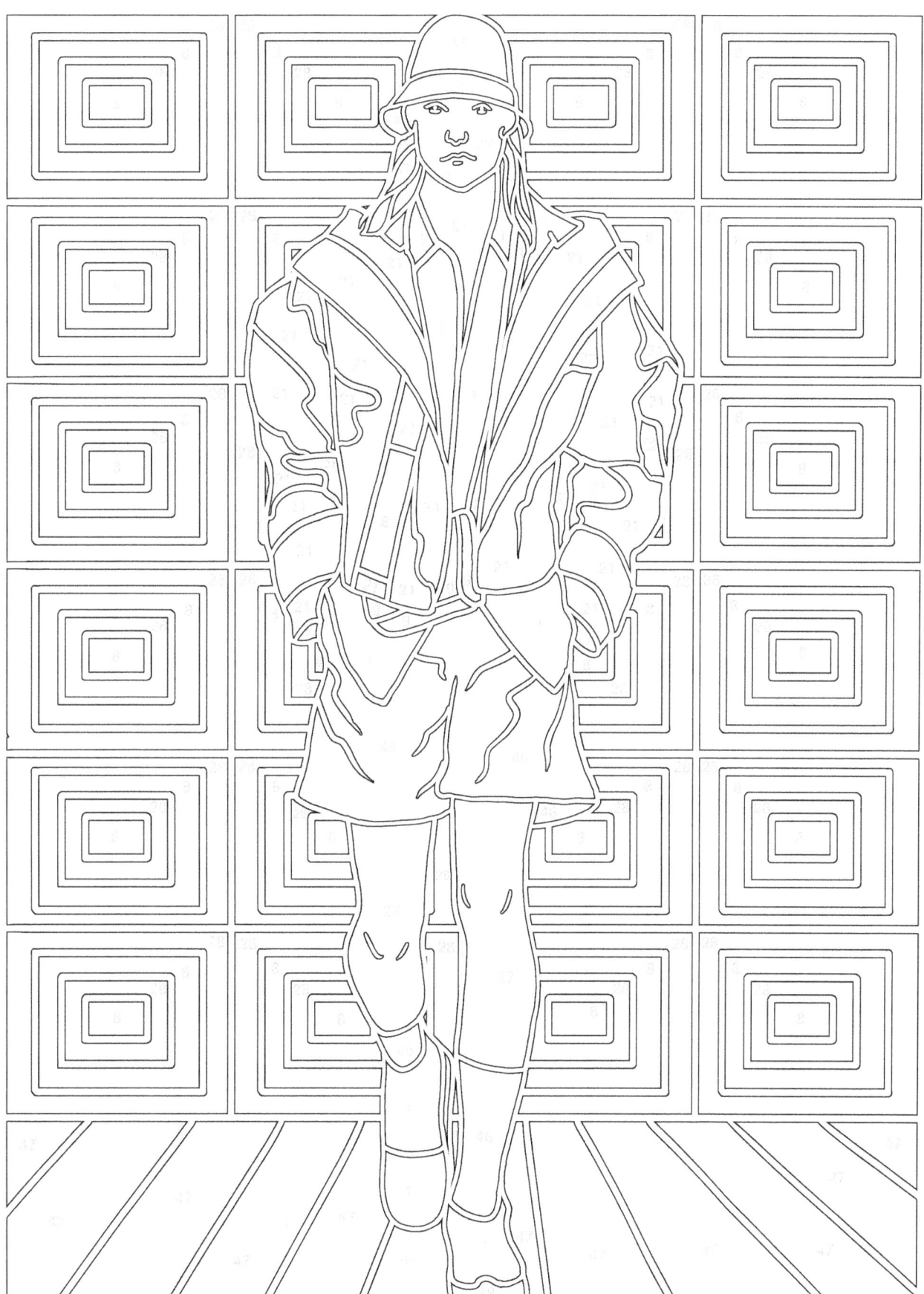

1. Black
2. Golden
3. Light Red
4. Medium Red
5. Red
6. Dark Red
7. Lemon Yellow
8. Light Yellow
9. Yellow
10. Dark Yellow
11. Bright Orange
12. Light Orange
13. Medium Orange
14. Orange
15. Dark Orange
16. Chocolate
17. Light Brown
18. Medium Brown
19. Brown
20. Dark Brown
21. Neon Green
22. Light Green
23. Medium Green
24. Green
25. Army Green
26. Dark Green
27. Peach
28. Light Pink
29. Medium Pink
30. Pink
31. Hot Pink
32. Dark Pink
33. Medium Purple
34. Purple
35. Light Violet
36. Soft Violet
37. Violet
38. Dark Violet
39. Baby Blue
40. Sky Blue
41. Light Blue
42. Medium Blue
43. Blue
44. Dark Blue
45. Navy Blue
46. Beige
47. Light Gray
48. Medium Gray
49. Gray
50. Dark Gray

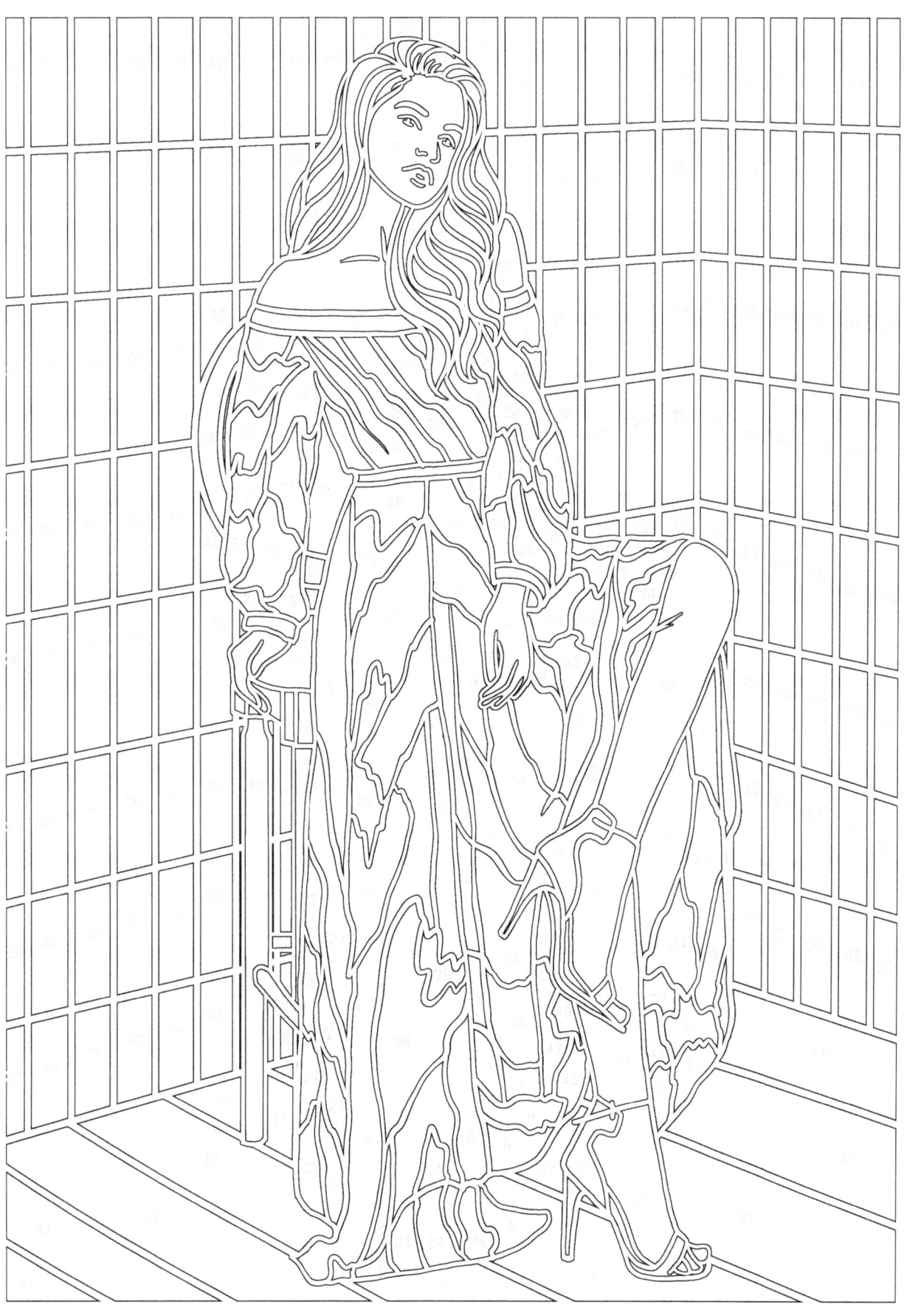

ENJOY BONUS
IMAGES FROM SOME
OF OUR
OTHER FUN
COLOR BY NUMBER
BOOKS!

FIND ALL OF OUR
BOOKS
ON AMAZON

BEAUTIFUL OCEAN
UNDER THE SEA
Easy Design
Color By Number
Coloring Book

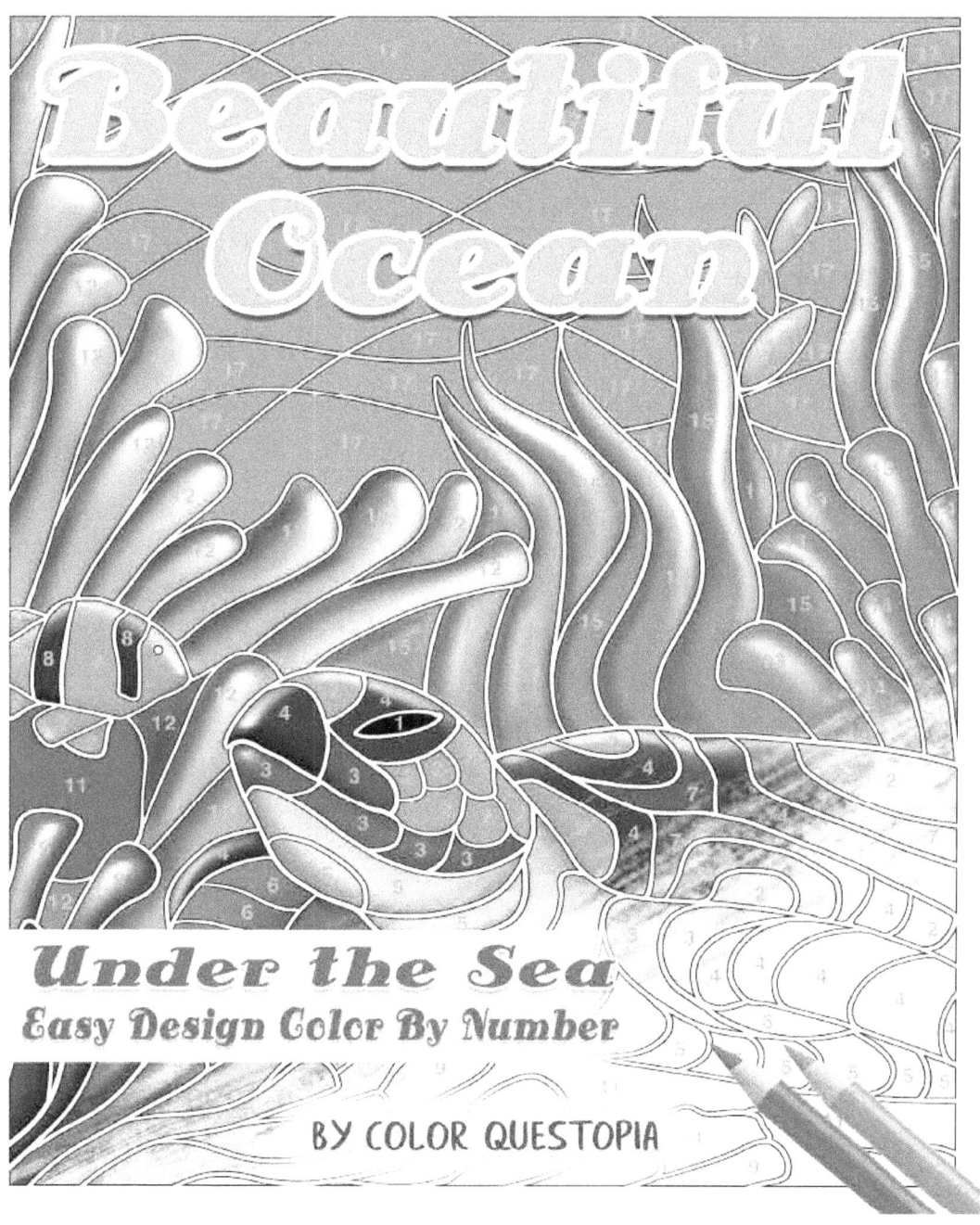

1. Black

2. Orange

3. Blue

4. Yellow

5. Violet

6. Light Violet

7. Light Orange

8. Light Red

9. Red

10. Light Pink

11. Pink

12. Light Brown

13. Green

14. Light Green

15. Purple

16. Light Purple

17. Light Green

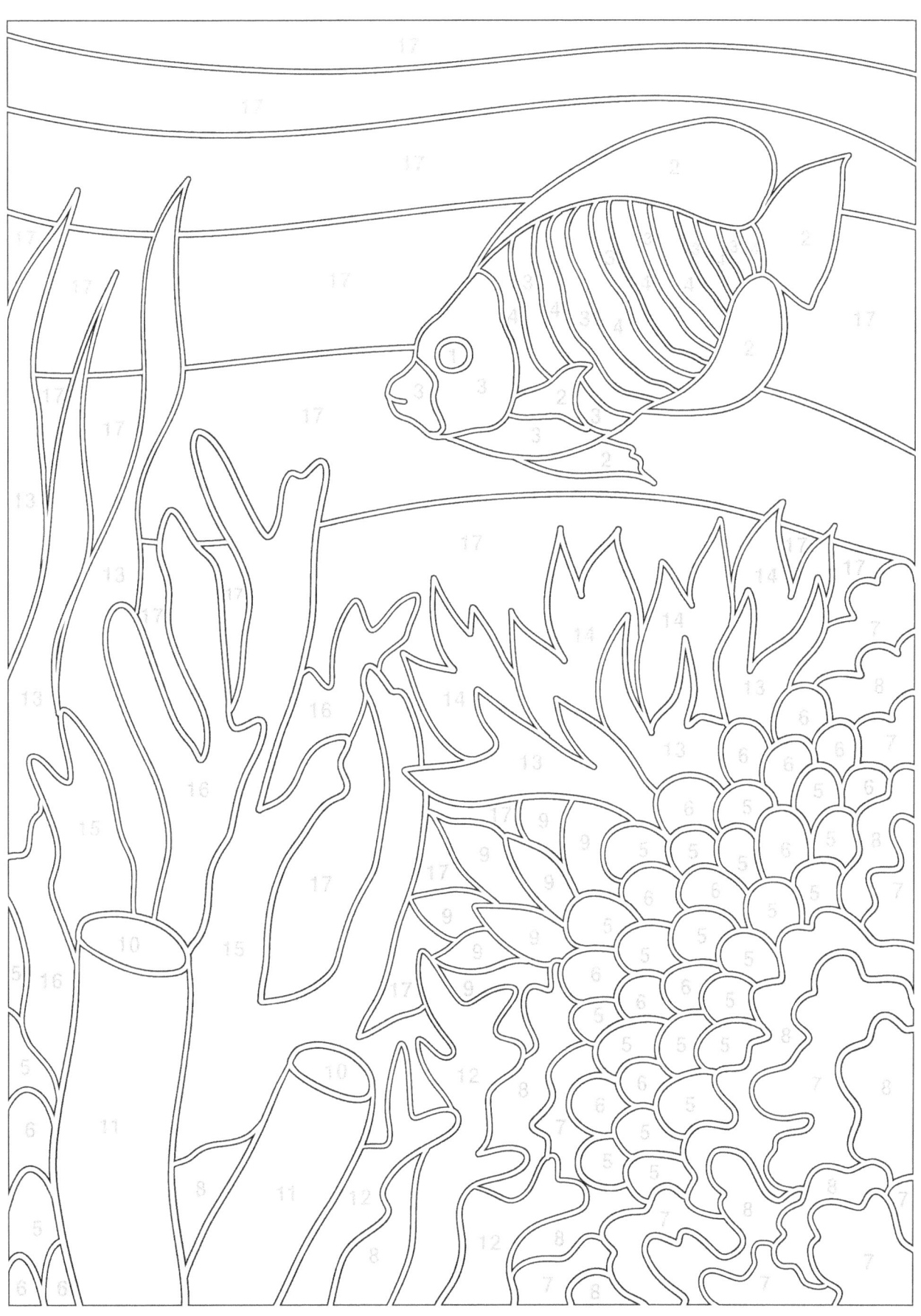

RACE CARS, MUSCLE CARS CLASSIC CARS
EASY DESIGN
MOSAIC BY NUMBER
COLORING BOOK

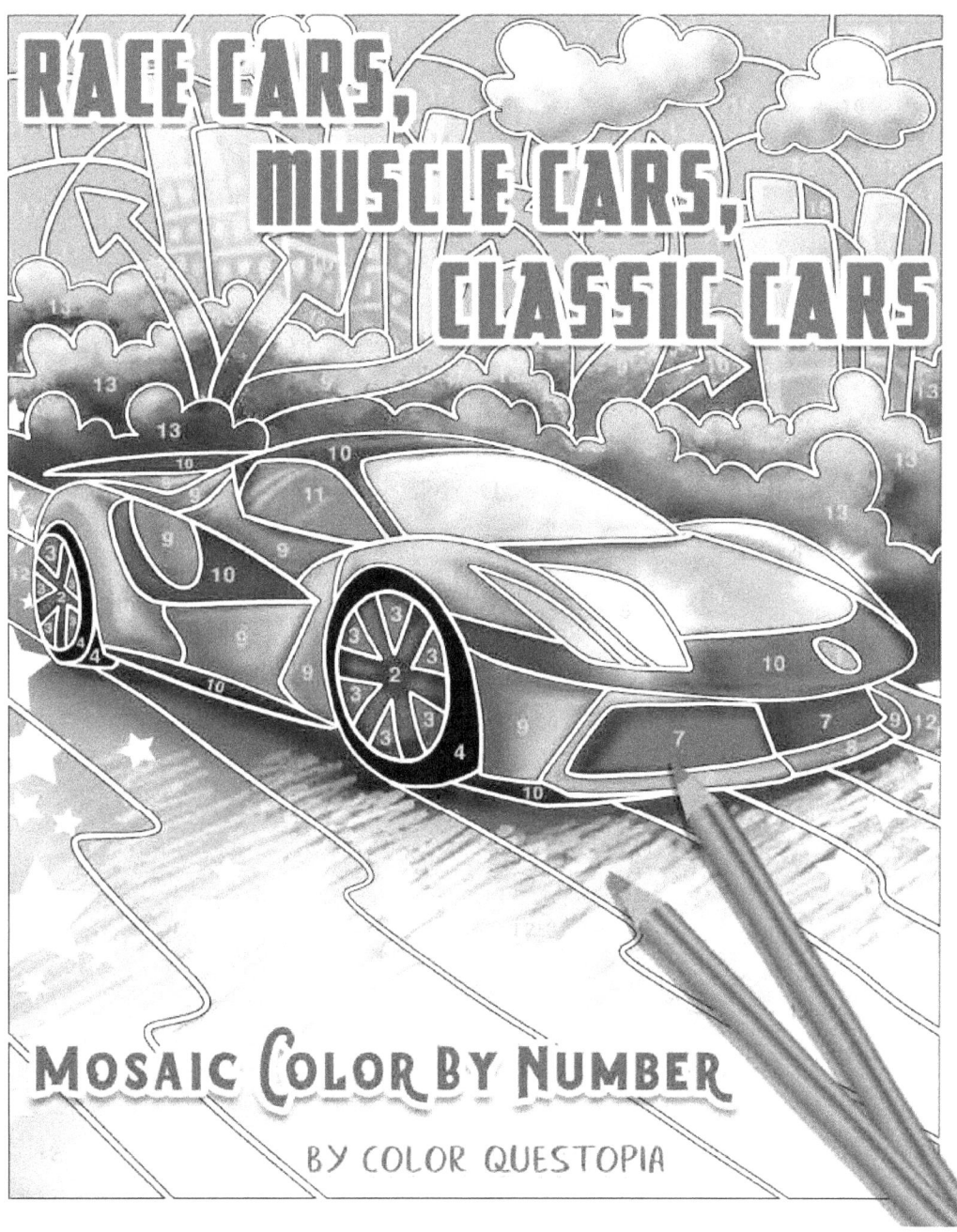

1. Black

2. Yellow

3. Light Green

4. Light Orange

5. Dark Orange

6. Dark Gray

7. Orange

8. Blue

9. Light Brown

10. Red

11. Gray

12. Pink

13. Light Violet

14. Light Gray

15. Light Blue

16. Dark Pink

17. Violet

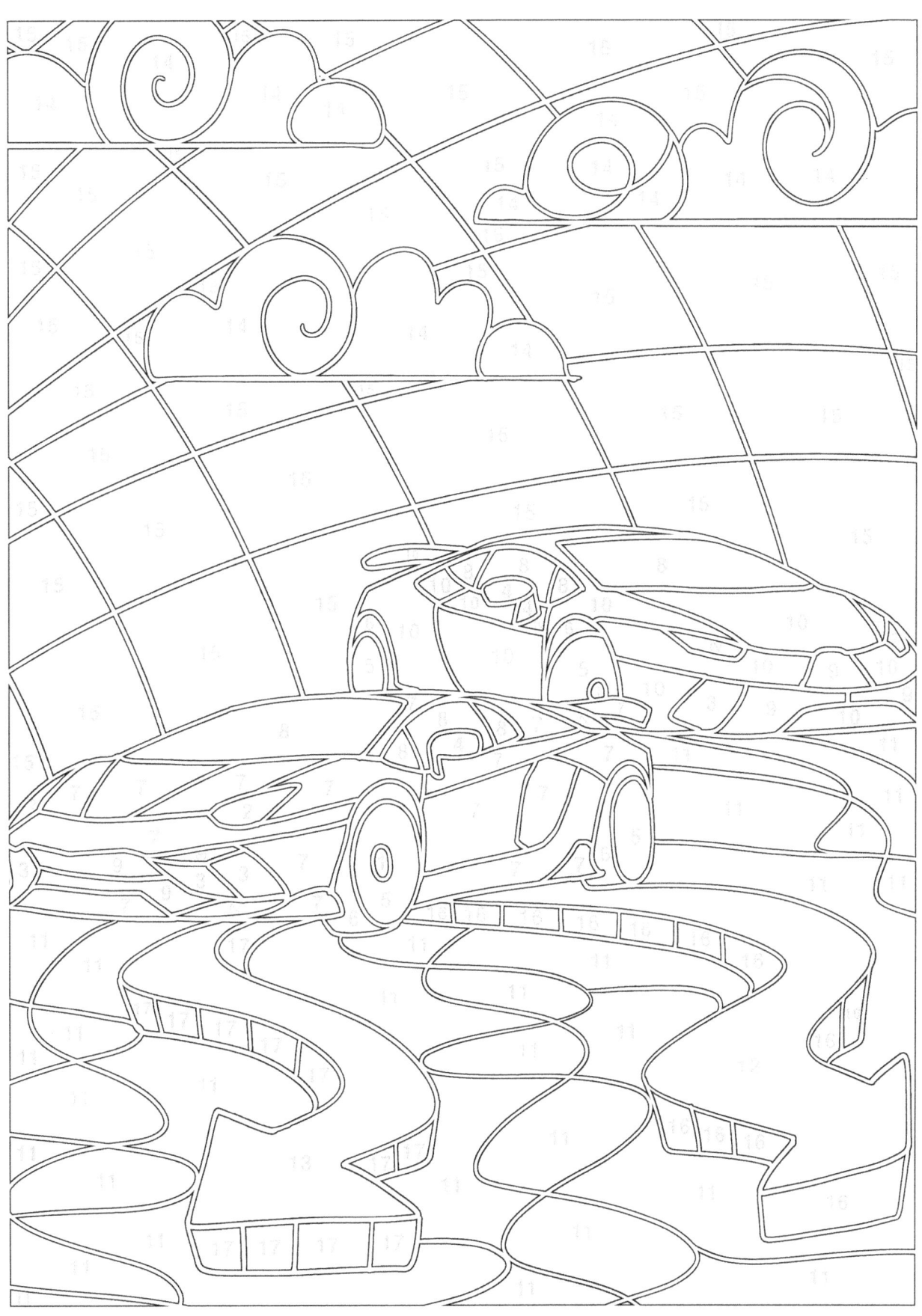

INCREDIBLE CATS AND KITTENS
Mosaic Color By Number
Adult Coloring Book

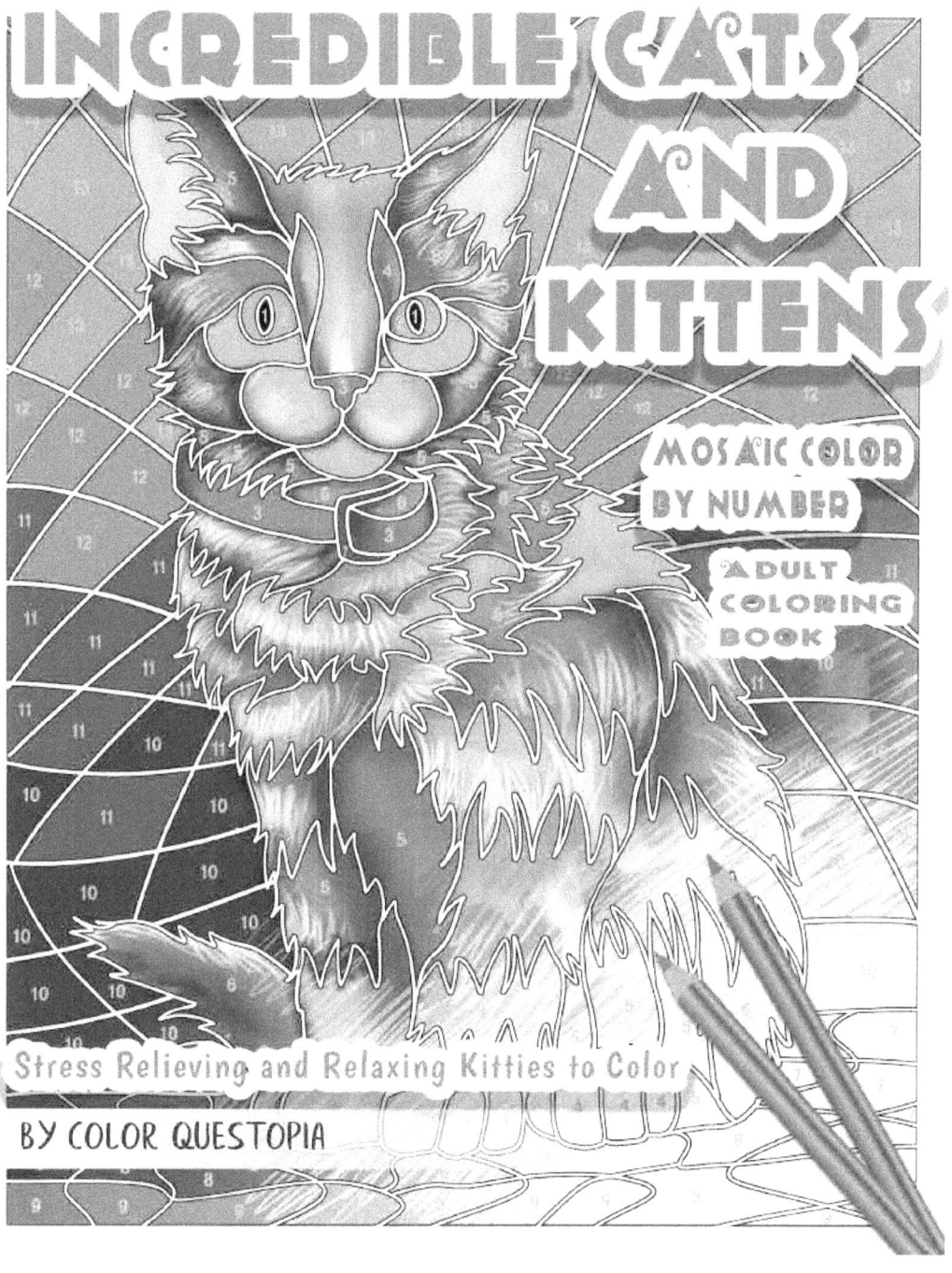

1. Black

2. Blue

3. Brown

4. Dark Yellow

5. Beige

6. Dark Gray

7. Gray

8. Light Gray

9. Green

10. Light Green

11. Neon Green

12. Sky Blue

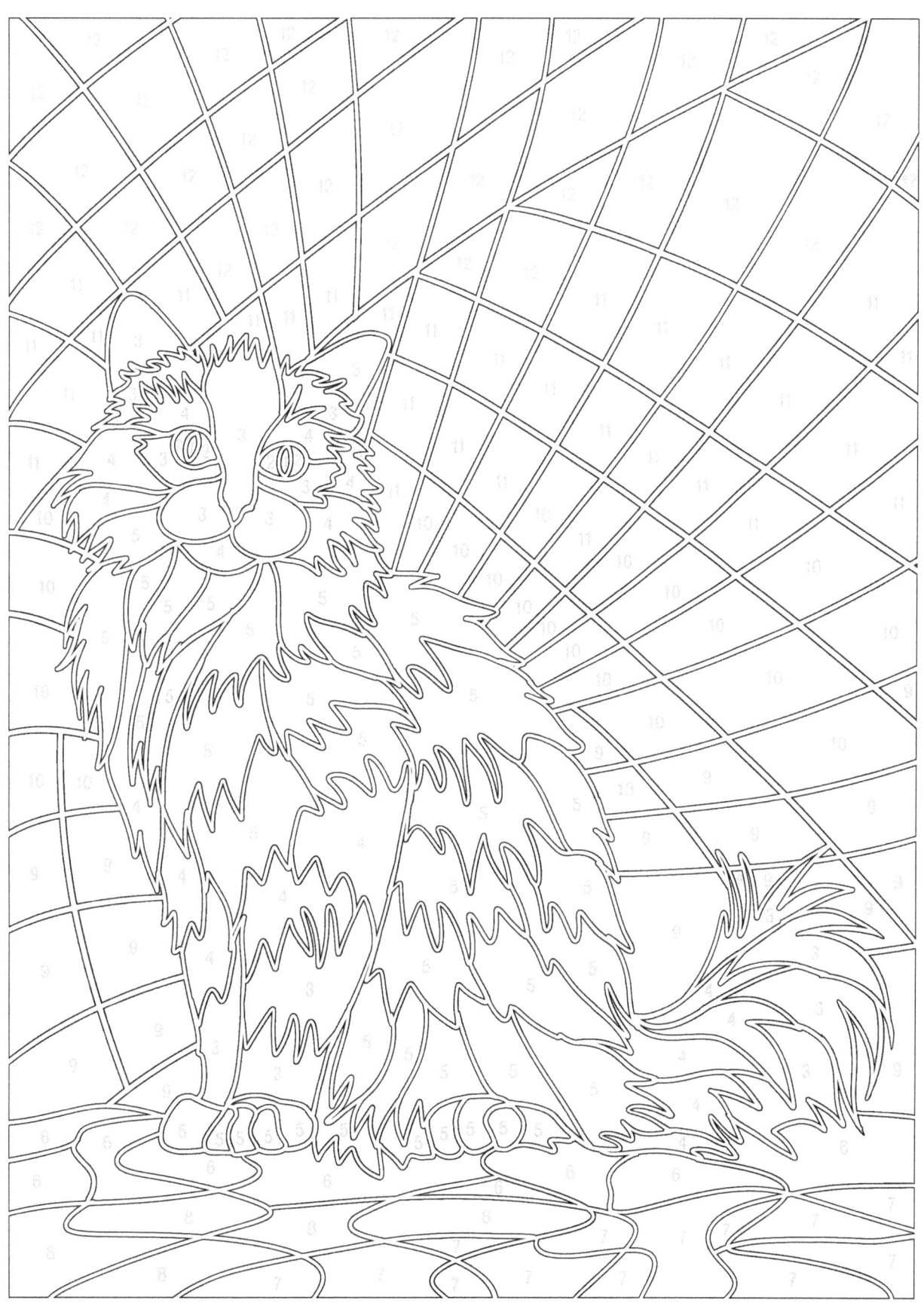

Candy Coloring Book
Delicious Mosiac Color By Number
Sweet Treats and Desserts

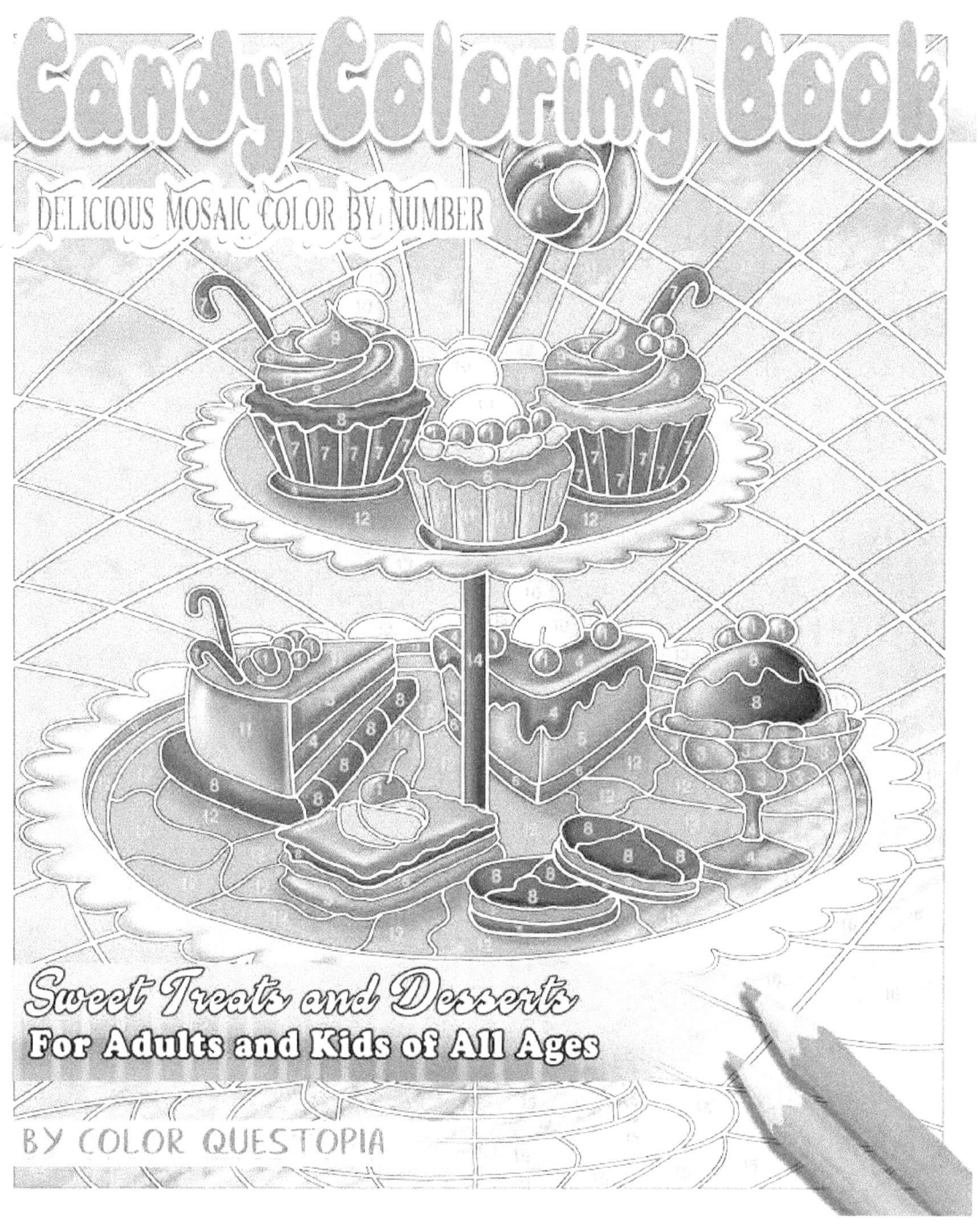

1. Light Orange
2. Red
3. Green
4. Dark Yellow
5. Yellow
6. Light Brown
7. Violet
8. Brown
9. Orange
10. Light Green
11. Medium Red
12. Light Yellow
13. Pink
14. Light Pink
15. Light Violet
16. Beige
17. Light Blue

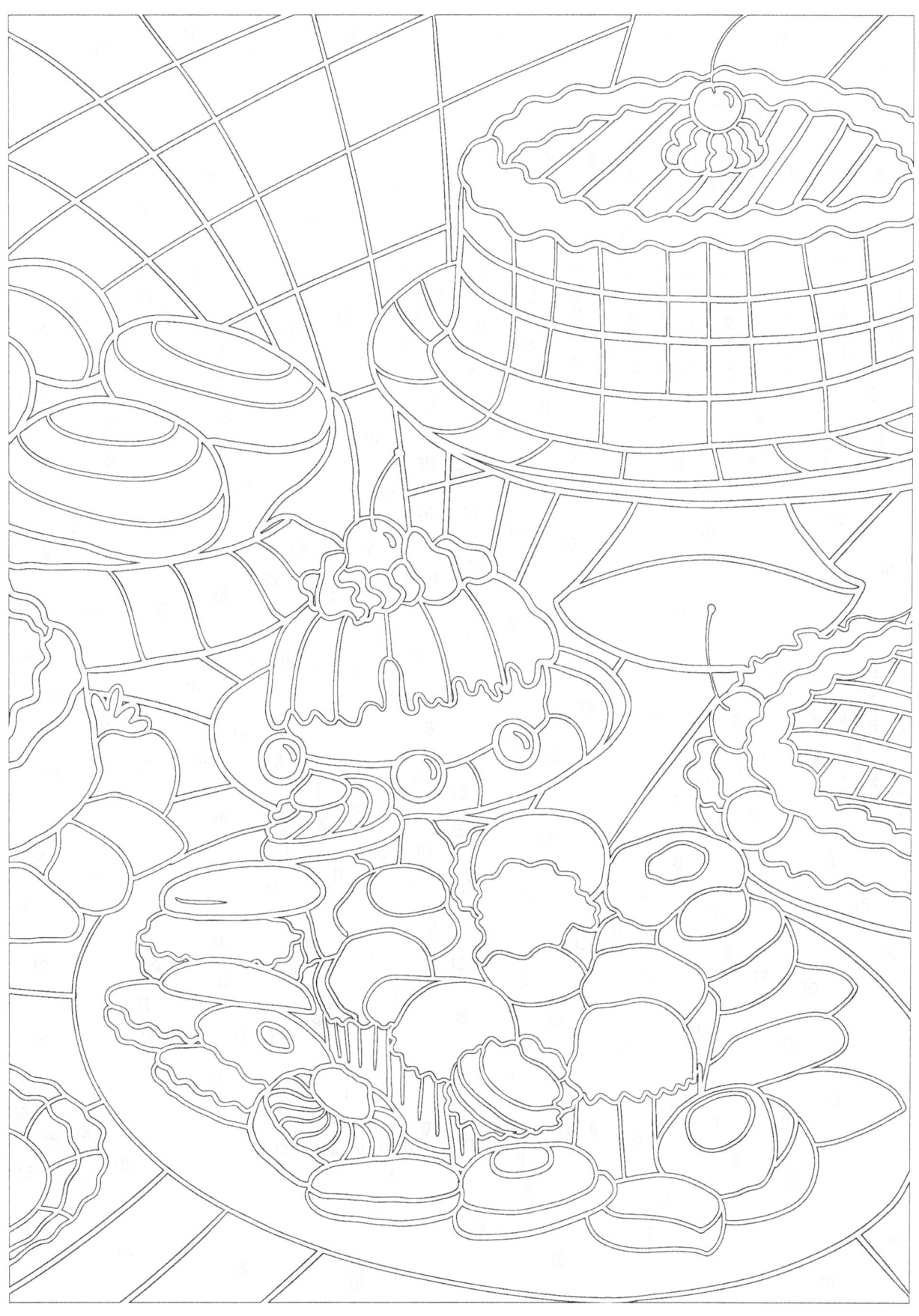

BEAUTIFUL PANDAS
Color By Number
A Mosaic Adult Coloring Book

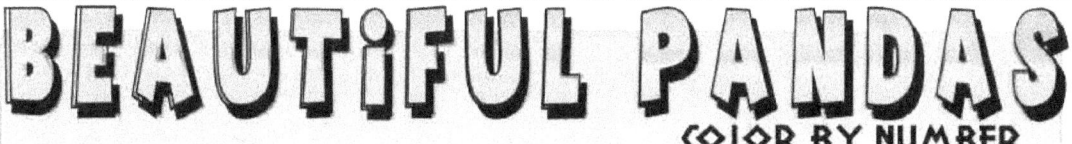

BEAUTIFUL PANDAS
COLOR BY NUMBER

A MOSAIC ADULT COLORING BOOK

BY COLOR QUESTOPIA

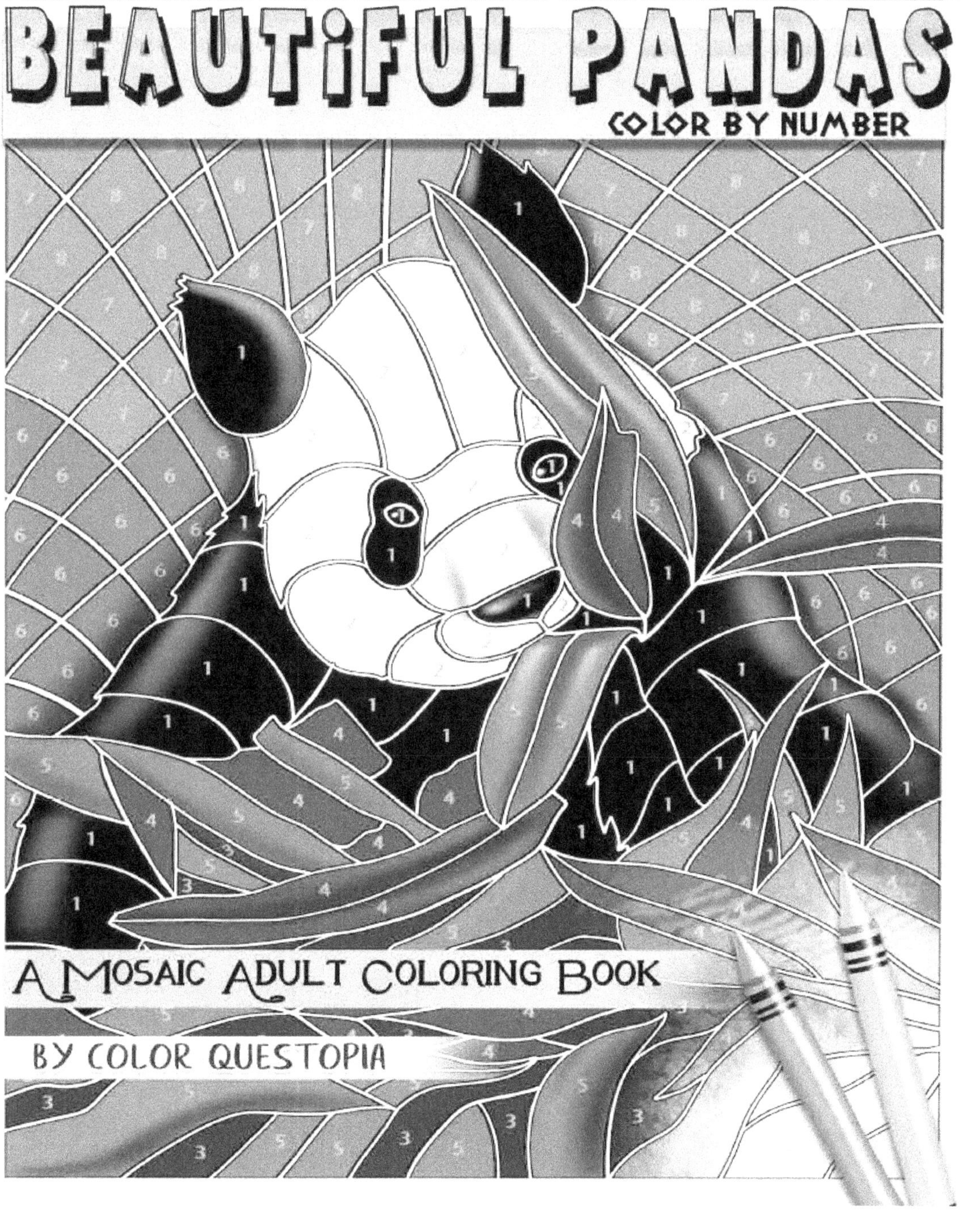

1. Black

2. White

3. Green

4. Light Brown

5. Medium Brown

6. Brown

7. Dark Green

8. Medium Green

9. Light Green

10. Neon Green

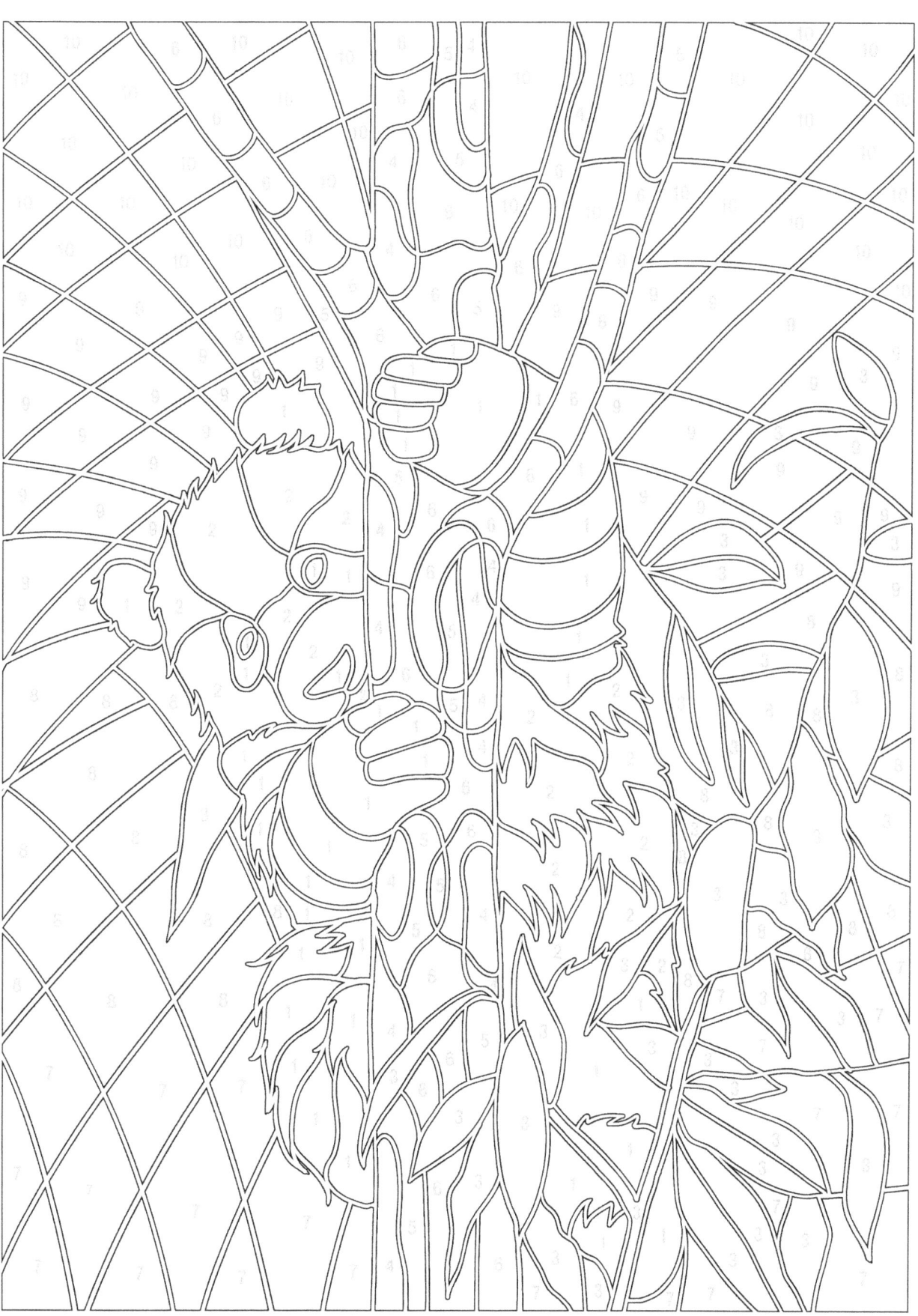

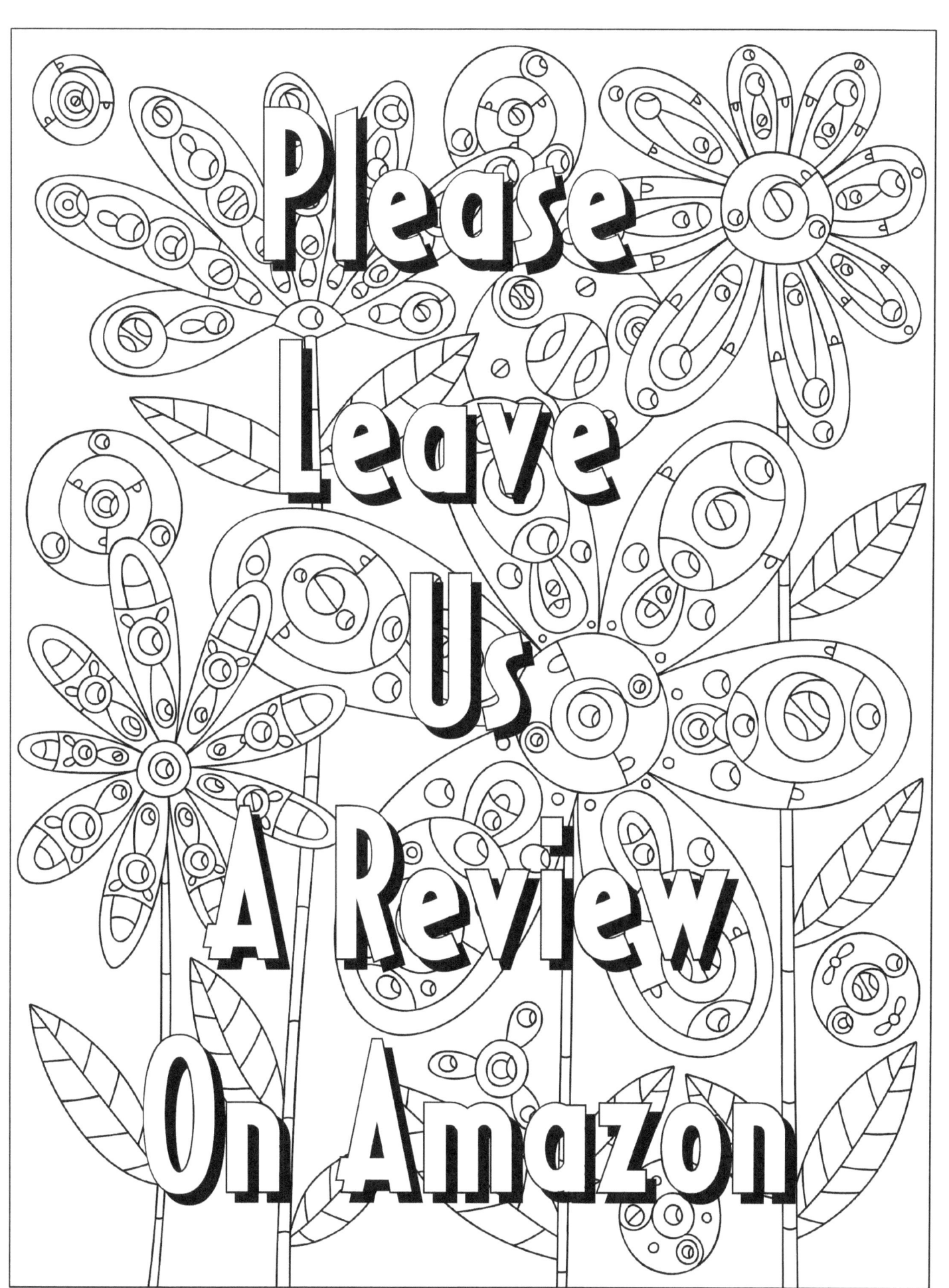

www.ingramcontent.com/pod-product-compliance
Lightning Source LLC
Chambersburg PA
CBHW080900220526
45467CB00008B/2574